# Hawks & Owls

## OF THE GREAT LAKES REGION & EASTERN NORTH AMERICA

Chris G. Earley

# Hawks & Owls

## OF THE GREAT LAKES REGION & EASTERN NORTH AMERICA

Chris G. Earley

FIREFLY BOOKS

# A FIREFLY BOOK

Published by Firefly Books Ltd. 2004

First Printing 2004

**Publisher Cataloging-in-Publication Data (U.S) (Library of Congress Standards)**

Earley, Chris G., 1968-
   Hawks and owls of the Great Lakes
   Region & eastern North America /
   Chris G. Earley. –1st ed.
[128] p. : col. photos. , maps ; cm.
Includes bibliographical references and index.
Summary: A field guide to over 30 species of birds of prey. Includes detailed descriptions of markings, flight characteristics, migration and plumage changes.
ISBN 1-55297-903-2
ISBN 1-55297-847-8  (pbk.)

1. Hawks – East (U.S.)
2. Owls – East (U.S.)
3. Hawks – Canada, Eastern.
4. Owls – Canada, Eastern.
5. Birds of prey – North America.
I. Title.

598.9/44/0974 21    QL696.F32E37 2004

**National Library of Canada Cataloguing in Publication Data**

Earley, Chris G., 1968-

Hawks and owls of the Great Lakes Region & eastern North America / Chris G. Earley.

Includes bibliographical references.
ISBN 1-55297-903-2 (bound).
ISBN 1-55297-847-8 (pbk.)

1. Hawks – Great Lakes Region.
2. Hawks – Canada, Eastern.
3. Hawks – East (U.S.)
4. Owls – Great Lakes Region.
5. Owls – Canada, Eastern.
6. Owls – East (U.S.)
I. Title.

QL696.F32E27 2004   598.9'44'09713
C2003-905565-5

Published in the U.S. in 2004 by
Firefly Books (U.S.) Inc.
P.O. Box 1338, Ellicott Station
Buffalo, New York 14205

Design by Lind Design
Printed and bound in Singapore
by Tien Wah Press (Pte) Ltd.

Published in Canada in 2004 by
Firefly Books Ltd.
66 Leek Crescent
Richmond Hill, Ontario L4B 1H1

Front cover photo: Jim Flynn
Back cover photo: Robert McCaw
Title page: Robert McCaw

*The Publisher acknowledges the financial support of the Government of Canada through the Book Publishing Industry Development Program for its publishing activities.*

# Table of Contents

# Those magnificent raptors

S EEING A HAWK RIDING LOFTY AIR CURRENTS OR
hearing an owl calling through the darkness is awe-
inspiring to most observers. Yet, while many of us find these
birds interesting, they can be a difficult group to identify.
Many hawks zip past us too quickly, and the nocturnal
habits of most owls leave us in the dark about their appearance. This book will help you identify these fascinating
birds as well as learn a bit about their natural history.

Watching birds
in their environ-
ment reveals
interactions that
link all of nature
together.

When trying to identify birds it is important to remember
the following motto: *I don't know*.

Really, it's okay to say it. Too many birders will get an incon-
clusive view of a bird and then just guess. With practice, you
can identify birds from incredibly short glimpses of them,
but there will always be some "I don't knows." And even if
you do get a good look and still can't identify the bird, you
will have learned from the process. The next time you see
that species, it will be familiar to you and you may see
another field mark or behavior to help in its identification.
And don't forget to watch the birds as well! Keeping a
checklist is fun and a way to record your sightings, but careful observations will help you really understand these interesting creatures. Watching birds in their environment
reveals interactions that link all of nature together.

# How to use this book

Size is a field mark that isn't very reliable; for example, many birds often look bigger when they are flying or perched on a dead tree. But because different hawk species may migrate together and may be seen chasing or eating known prey species, size comparisons can be made. As well, both hawks and owls are often "mobbed" by small birds, offering another chance for size comparison. In this book, the raptor's length and wingspan are compared to those of a well-known species, with the measurement indicated as fairly equal to (=), less than (<) or greater than (>) the well-known bird. Average measurements for these species are given below. Remember that there are always individual variations; also, except for vultures, the females of each species described in this book are commonly larger than the males.

| Length | | | |
|---|---|---|---|
| American Robin | 10″ (25 cm) | Red-tailed Hawk | 19″ (48 cm) |
| Rock Pigeon | 13″ (33 cm) | Bald Eagle | 31″ (79 cm) |
| American Crow | 17″ (43 cm) | | |
| **Wingspan** | | | |
| Mourning Dove | 18″ (46 cm) | Red-tailed Hawk | 49″ (124 cm) |
| Killdeer | 24″ (61 cm) | Herring Gull | 58″ (147 cm) |
| Rock Pigeon | 28″ (71 cm) | Great Blue Heron | 72″ (183 cm) |
| American Crow | 39″ (99 cm) | | |

**= PERCHED**  A description of the shape and field marks of a sitting hawk or owl.

**= IN FLIGHT**  A description of field marks to help identify a hawk flying overhead; unless otherwise noted, these descriptions relate to the underparts of the bird.

**ADULT**  Birds that have reached their adult plumage. This may be achieved by their first fall, or near their second fall, or not until four to six years of age, depending on the species.

The box at the top left of the page graphically represents the adult female hawk's or eagle's undertail coverts and tail pattern. For owls, there is a silhouette of the owl's shape and size.

**FIRST YEAR**

Birds that have not reached their adult plumage. Typically, most hawks have a first year plumage that lasts until the bird is approximately one year old. Eagles have additional plumages before they acquire their full adult plumage.

**FLEDGLING/ FIRST FALL**

Birds that have a plumage that is distinctive for a few months after they leave the nest.

**MORPH**

Some hawk and owl species have more than one color morph. This is not related to the sex or age of an individual or to seasonal changes; it is their color for life. This is comparable to the gray or black colors of gray squirrels or the yellow, chocolate or black colors of Labrador Retrievers.

**FLIGHT TRAITS**

A description of shape, behavior or flight patterns that may help identify a species.

**LISTEN FOR**

Learning and remembering owl calls is an important skill for identifying this group of birds, since they are more often heard than seen. Hawks also have distinctive calls, but are harder to distinguish. Only one or two examples of common calls are given here. Listening to recordings of bird calls will help you hone your recognition skills.

**COMPARE TO**

This lists other birds that look similar to the particular hawk or owl. Comparison pages at the back of the book will be helpful when comparing similar species.

**SEASONAL STATUS**

This list (page 17) refers to the seasonal status of hawks and owls at Point Pelee National Park. Because Point Pelee is a central point for much of the Great Lakes region, you can use this information as a guideline for when these birds may arrive or leave your area. However, because Point Pelee may not have the breeding or wintering habitat required for many species, the application of this chart during the summer and winter may be less accurate for your area.

**RANGE MAPS**

These maps show each species' breeding and wintering ranges, as well as where they may be resident all year long.

# A note to beginners

Watch the bird for a while before flipping through this guide.

WHEN LOOKING AT HAWKS, resist the urge to instantly start flipping through this guide. Watch the bird first. This way you can look for field marks and behaviors before the bird disappears from your view. Ask yourself questions such as *Does it have pointed wings or rounded wings? Are there any markings on its breast or belly? Does it have a long or short tail? What markings does it have on its wings?*

Once you've answered these and other questions, then look in this book. A hawk flying overhead doesn't always stay in view for long and you should spend your time looking at it before it moves on.

Try to learn the common species of your area first. Don't just observe their markings – recognize their shapes and flight patterns, too. Being familiar with the common hawks will help with identification of the less common or migratory species that you will come across.

# The quotes

MANY OF THE DESCRIPTIONS in this book include a quote from naturalist writings on bird behavior and identification. While these observations may seem unscientific or "fluffy" to some readers, I believe that these naturalists have a magnificent understanding of birds and their lives. While giving nonhuman creatures human characteristics (anthropomorphism) is unscientific, I believe that beginners can benefit from this practice. What better way for a human to initially learn about something than to use humanlike descriptions? So try reading the quotes, then watch a hawk hunting or listen to an owl calling. You may find that the melodramatic or colorful style does indeed apply to your subject.

While giving nonhuman creatures human characteristics is unscientific, beginners can benefit from this practice.

# Taxonomy

YOU MAY BE SURPRISED to learn that many raptor species are not very closely related (see next page). In fact, owls are more closely related to whip-poor-wills than they are to hawks. Even more surprising is the new classification that puts the Turkey Vulture within the same group as storks. This may seem confusing, but keep in mind that many different bird groups eat other creatures. Most of the birds in this book have adapted to using their strong talons to catch their food.

Surprisingly, many raptor species are not very closely related.

The order of the birds in this book follows the seventh edition of the *American Ornithologists' Union Check-list of North American Birds*. The birds are arranged in a specific sequence (taxonomic order) that recognizes relationships between species. You may notice that many closely related birds, such as the Accipiter hawks, will have similar behaviors, shapes and flight patterns. This will hopefully help you to use shape and behavior as identification aids.

# Classification of the birds in this book

HERE IS A LIST that shows how the birds in this book are classified. Each genus in a family is listed to show which species are quite closely related.

**Class Aves: Birds**
**Order Ciconiiformes: Herons, Ibises, Storks & New World Vultures**

**FAMILY CATHARTIDAE: NEW WORLD VULTURES**

| Genus | | |
|---|---|---|
| | *Coragyps* | Black Vulture |
| | *Cathartes* | Turkey Vulture |

**Order Falconiformes: The Diurnal Birds of Prey**

**FAMILY ACCIPITRIDAE: OSPREY, KITES, EAGLES, HAWKS & ALLIES**

| Genus | | |
|---|---|---|
| | *Pandion* | Osprey |
| | *Elanoides* | Swallow-tailed Kite |
| | *Ictinia* | Mississippi Kite |
| | *Haliaeetus* | Bald Eagle |
| | *Circus* | Northern Harrier |
| | *Accipiter* | Northern Goshawk, Sharp-shinned & Cooper's Hawks |
| | *Buteo* | Red-shouldered, Broad-winged, Swainson's, Red-tailed, Ferruginous & Rough-legged Hawks |
| | *Aquila* | Golden Eagle |

**FAMILY FALCONIDAE: CARACARAS & FALCONS**

| Genus | | |
|---|---|---|
| | *Falco* | American Kestrel, Merlin, Gyrfalcon, Peregrine Falcon & Prairie Falcon |

**Order Strigiformes: Owls**

**FAMILY TYTONIDAE: BARN & BAY OWLS**

| Genus | | |
|---|---|---|
| | *Tyto* | Barn Owl |

**FAMILY STRIGIDAE: TYPICAL OWLS**

| Genus | | |
|---|---|---|
| | *Megascops* | Eastern Screech-Owl |
| | *Bubo* | Great Horned Owl & Snowy Owl |
| | *Surnia* | Northern Hawk Owl |
| | *Strix* | Barred & Great Gray Owls |
| | *Asio* | Long-eared & Short-eared Owls |
| | *Aegolius* | Boreal & Northern Saw-whet Owls |

# Hawk groups

HAWKS IN THE SAME GENUS share similar shapes that can be recognized in the field, allowing birders to narrow down what species they are looking at by noticing the overall shape first. Here are a few examples; others are discussed in the text for each species.

Sharp-shinned

**Accipiters (Sharp-shinned, Cooper's & Northern Goshawk)**
Overall these hawks have relatively short, rounded wings and long tails – adaptations for quick bursts of speed and fine maneuverability when chasing smaller birds through forested areas.

**Buteos (Red-tailed, Rough-legged, Broad-winged, Swainson's, Ferruginous & Red-shouldered)**
These hawks have long, rounded, wide wings and relatively short tails – adaptations for soaring to look for prey. Some of these characteristics are also found in vultures and eagles.

Red-tailed

**Northern Harrier**
This species has long, rounded wings and a long tail. It coasts close to the ground while looking for small mammalian prey.

Harrier

**Osprey**
This species has long wings that are usually held with a bend at the wrist, giving the Osprey a distinctive shape.

Osprey

**Falcons (American Kestrel, Merlin, Peregrine, Prairie & Gyrfalcon)**
These hawks have long, pointed wings for fast flying to chase down prey in open areas. Mississippi and Swallow-tailed Kites also have this wing shape.

All of these hawks can modify their shape depending on whether they are *soaring* (wings out fully with completely spread wing tips and tail feathers) or *gliding* (wings somewhat bent and wing tips and tail feathers folded). Thus, a soaring Peregrine Falcon looks unfalconlike, whereas a Northern Goshawk in a glide looks quite falconlike. So, be careful when trying to put a hawk into one group or another.

Merlin

# Identification features

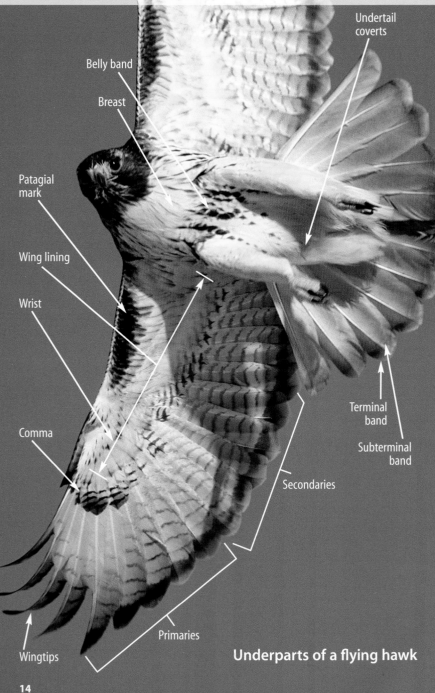

Undertail coverts

Belly band

Breast

Patagial mark

Wing lining

Wrist

Comma

Terminal band

Subterminal band

Secondaries

Primaries

Wingtips

**Underparts of a flying hawk**

Breast with streaking – vertical lines    WHEELER

Breast with barring – horizontal lines    FLYNN

Ear tuft   Eyebrow   Mustache   Facial disk

Owl facial features    McCAW

Primaries

Secondaries

Rump

Leading edge of wing

Trailing edge of wing

Upperparts    WHEELER

# Hawk look-alikes

OWLS ARE QUITE DISTINCTIVE due to their large heads, but hawks have a few look-alikes that sometimes confuse the observer.

McCAW

Flying terns, gulls (such as this Herring Gull) and nighthawks can sometimes look like falcons or kites because of their pointed wings, but gulls have a long beak and nighthawks have white wing patches.

SMALL

The fast flight and pointed wings of the Rock pigeon, shown here, can make it appear to be a Merlin or Peregrine to beginning birders. The Mourning Dove has a display flight that can look surprisingly similar to a gliding Sharp-shinned Hawk.

McCAW

Northern (shown) and Loggerhead Shrikes are raptorial songbirds with hooked beaks that use their feet to catch their prey.

McCAW

More than once I've had people bring me a window-killed "hawk" that ended up being a Ruffed Grouse.

Another to be aware of is the Common Raven, which is a hawk-sized "songbird" that often soars – watch for its wedge-shaped tail. American Crows, Killdeer and Purple Martins can all do a good hawk or falcon imitation, too.

# Seasonal status of hawks & owls
## for Point Pelee National Park

| ■ Common | ▥ Uncommon | — Rare | ····· Very rare |

| Month | J | F | M | A | M | J | J | A | S | O | N | D |
|---|---|---|---|---|---|---|---|---|---|---|---|---|
| Black Vulture | | | · | | · | | | · | | | | |
| Turkey Vulture | · | · | ·— | ▥▥ | ▥— | | | | ▥ | ■ | — | ····· |
| Osprey | | | | — | —·· | | ·· | | —▥ | ▥— | · ·· | |
| Swallow-tailed Kite | | | | | · · | | | ···· | | | | |
| Mississippi Kite | | | | | ···· | | | | | | | |
| Bald Eagle | ▮ | — | ▥ | | | | | | | | | |
| Northern Harrier | — | | ▥ | ▥ | ▥— | | | — | ■ | | — | |
| Sharp-shinned Hawk | — | | | ▥ | ▥— | · | —··· | ····· | — | ■ | — | |
| Cooper's Hawk | — | | | | | | ·········· | | — | ▥ ■ | — | |
| Northern Goshawk | — | | | ···· | · | | | · —··· | — | | | |
| Red-shouldered Hawk | — | | | | | | | | — | ▥ | ▥ | |
| Broad-winged Hawk | | | | ·· | ▥ | ·—····· | | · | —▥ | ■ | ·· | |
| Swainson's Hawk | | | | · · | | | | | | | | |
| Red-tailed Hawk | ▥ | ▥ | ▥ | — | | | | — | ▥ | ■ | — | |
| Rough-legged Hawk | ▥ | ▥ | ▥ | ▥— | | | | · | · · | ▥ | | |
| Golden Eagle | · | · | ·· | ···· | | · | | ·· | · ··· | | | ·· |
| American Kestrel | ▥ | ▥ | ▥ | ▥ | ▥— | | | ■ | — | | | |
| Merlin | | · | ···· | — | | | | ·· | ▥ | — | · | · |
| Gyrfalcon | | · | | · | | | | | | | | |
| Peregrine Falcon | | | ····· | —··· | | | | ·· | ▥ | — | | · |
| Barn Owl | | ······················ | | | | | | · | · · | — | | |
| Eastern Screech-Owl | ▥▥▥▥▥▥▥▥▥▥▥▥▥▥▥▥▥▥▥▥▥▥▥ |
| Great Horned Owl | ▥▥▥▥▥▥▥▥▥▥▥▥▥▥▥▥▥▥▥▥▥▥▥ |
| Snowy Owl | — | | · | ··· | | | | | | — | | |
| Long-eared Owl | — | | | | ·· | | | | | — | | |
| Short-eared Owl | — | | | ··· | | | · | · | — | | | |
| Northern Saw-whet Owl | — | | | · | | | | | — | ▥ | | |

FROM J.R. GRAHAM 1996

Adult                                                                      REAUME

THE BLACK VULTURE IS FOUND from the southeastern U.S. all the way through Mexico and most of Central and South America. It is a rare wanderer to the Great Lakes region. Unlike Turkey Vultures, Black Vultures can't find carrion by smell. To compensate for this, they keep a sharp eye out for descending Turkey Vultures, which can smell carcasses hidden from above by trees or shrubs. Once at the carcass, the more aggressive Black Vultures often chase the Turkey Vultures away and get to feed first.

## SIZE

Length > Red-tailed Hawk
Wingspan = Herring Gull

### ADULT

*Naked gray head* • long beak with light tip • all black body • short tail • gray legs.

### FLIGHT TRAITS

Wide wings held at slight dihedral when soaring • when it flaps, the *wing beats are fast and shallow* • *short, triangular tail.*

### ADULT

*Small, naked gray head* • *light gray primaries contrasting with the rest of the black wings and body.*

### FIRST YEAR

Similar to adult except for • blackish head with no light tip on beak.

Adult                                    FLYNN

This partial albino Turkey Vulture has     FLYNN
a similar pattern to the Black Vulture, but
note the difference in shape.

## LISTEN FOR

Hisses and grunts when interacting with other vultures at a carcass.

## COMPARE TO

Turkey Vulture, Golden and Bald Eagles.

## NATURE NOTES

Like other New World vultures, Black Vultures practice "urohidrosis," a big word that means they poop on their legs to stay cool. Unlike most of the birds in this book, this species is very social and family members may form groups that jointly defend roosts and carcasses from unrelated intruders.

**RANGE**

▨ Resident year round

## *Cathartes aura*

**Adult** — McCAW

**First fall** — WHEELER

HERE IS A BIRD THAT IS OFTEN described as ugly, but just as often described as beautiful. Its red, wrinkled, naked head may be unappealing to some observers, but its flight certainly makes up for it. A Turkey Vulture gracefully wafting through the air on its upheld wings is attractive to most earth-bound humans. This species uses its nonflapping flight to slowly coast around while its exceptional sense of smell hones in on its favorite food – dead animals. When a carcass is found, the reason for the Turkey Vulture's naked head becomes apparent as soon as the bird reaches inside for the good bits. Bird heads are difficult to self-preen, so the lack of head feathers is a great adaptation utilized by many carrion-eating species. Winsor Marrett Tyler (in Bent, 1937) describes it as "a naked head and neck like the bare arms of a butcher."

### SIZE

Length > Red-tailed Hawk
Wingspan < Great Blue Heron

Adult

SMALL

Note that the wings are held in a "V."

FLYNN

## ADULT

*Naked red head* • long white-tipped beak
• *blackish body* • some brown wash or
edging on back and wings • long tail
• pale pinkish legs.

## FLIGHT TRAITS

*Soars with wings in a strong dihedral or "V"*
• rocking or teetering flight • when it
flaps, the wing beats are deep and heavy
• *long tail*.

### RANGE

■ Breeding only
■ Resident year round

Adult

## ADULT

*Small, naked red head • gray flight feathers contrast with black wing linings and body.*

## FIRST YEAR

Similar to adult except for • some dusky coloration on the head and tip of the beak.

## FLEDGLING/FIRST FALL

Similar to first year except for • all gray head and dark beak tip.

## LISTEN FOR

Usually silent, but can hiss when interacting with other vultures at a carcass or when disturbed at its nest.

## COMPARE TO

Black Vulture, Golden and immature Bald Eagles.

## NATURE NOTES

Perched Turkey Vultures regularly spread their wings out and sun themselves. This is thought to help maintain body temperature and/or help feathers bend back into a normal shape after being bent when soaring. It may also aid in deterring parasites. One of their defence tactics when disturbed at the nest is to regurgitate, and they have also been known to "play dead."

Roosting adults

McCAW

This individual is sunning itself, a practice that may deter parasites or help feathers keep their shape.

SMALL

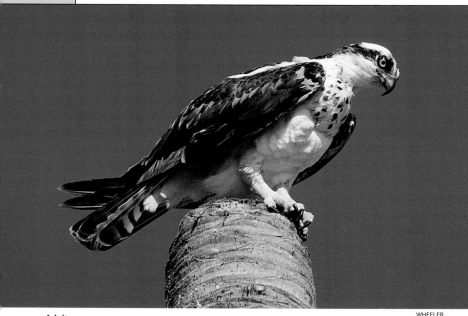

Adult

CATCHING FISH IS THE OSPREY'S specialty, often earning it the name of Fish Hawk. They hover above a potential meal and then plunge feet-first into the water, sometimes submerging themselves in the process. An outer toe that can rotate to the back and feet that are covered in tiny spines help the Osprey to grasp a slippery fish. When it clears the water's surface and starts for a suitable feeding perch, an Osprey often holds its catch so the fish's head and tail are oriented in the same way as the bird. This reduces drag, a helpful strategy when carrying an already heavy fish. But Osprey don't always catch a fish at each attempt. Studer (1881) wrote, "Their peculiar mode of fishing necessitates the making of many a plunge to no purpose; but this does not at all discourage them: their motto always is 'try again.'"

Adult

FLYNN

## SIZE

Length > Red-tailed Hawk
Wingspan > Herring Gull

## ⚑ ADULT

*White head* • *thick, dark brown eyeline*
• dark beak • dark brown upperparts
• *white underparts* • variable streaky dark
necklace on breast (usually more
apparent on females) • finely barred tail.

## FLIGHT TRAITS

Long wings held in a downward curve
(producing a shallow "M") • *wings may
bend at the wrist (like a gull)* • may hover
while hunting.

## ◣ ADULT

*White underparts* • possible streaked
necklace • heavily barred flight feathers,

### RANGE

■ Breeding only
■ Resident year round
□ Wintering only

25

Crows, jays and other birds often harrass or "mob" birds of prey.

FLYNN

especially on secondaries • *dark wrist patches* • dark wing tips • finely barred tail.

### FLEDGLING/FIRST FALL

Similar to adult except for • whitish edging on back and upperwings • may have buffy wash on underparts.

### LISTEN FOR

High, shrill whistles and chirps.

### COMPARE TO

Gulls, Bald Eagle, Rough-legged Hawk.

### NATURE NOTES

The Osprey can be found over much of the planet but is absent from the Arctic and Antarctica. There are reports of Ospreys attempting to catch fish that are too big and drowning because they can't free their talons from their prey.

Osprey may totally submerge when trying to catch a fish.

FLYNN

This osprey is trying to orient the fish's head forward to reduce drag.

REAUME

**Adult with chicks**

REAUME

Adult

"THE KITE COURSES THROUGH the air with a grace and buoyancy it would be vain to rival. By a stroke of the thin-bladed wings and a lashing of the cleft tail, its flight is swayed to this or that side in a moment ... it swoops with incredible swiftness." So wrote Coues (in Studer, 1881) and, indeed, this raptor is like a giant swallow, both in shape and elegance. It is rare in our area, but it sometimes does wander this far north, much to the delight of Great Lakes region birders.

### SIZE

Length > Red-tailed Hawk
Wingspan = Red-tailed Hawk

### ADULT

All white head • white underparts • shiny black back, wings and tail • very long, pointed wings and tail.

### FLIGHT TRAITS

*Long, pointed wings • very graceful flight • long, forked tail.*

### ADULT

All white head, underparts and wing linings • black back, primaries, secondaries and tail feathers.

### FLEDGLING/FIRST FALL

Similar to adult except for • shorter tail.

Adult                                                    WHEELER

Adult                          FLYNN

## LISTEN FOR

A high, whistled *kwee-kwee-kwee-kwee*.

## NATURE NOTES

The Swallow-tailed Kite has been known
to take entire small bird's nests containing
young and eat the nestlings as it flies
along.

**RANGE**

■ Breeding only
■ Resident year round

**Adult male** WHEELER

THE MISSISSIPPI KITE IS ANOTHER graceful flyer. Audubon (1840) wrote, "At times it floats in the air as if motionless, or sails in broad regular circles, when, suddenly closing its wings, it slides along to some distance, and renews its curves." The Mississippi Kite is found in the southern U.S., but is rare in the Great Lakes region. When seen here, it is usually during either spring or fall migration when some individuals may wander from their regular range.

### SIZE

Length > Rock Pigeon
Wingspan > Rock Pigeon

### ADULT MALE

*Pale gray head* • black patch in front of eye • *gray back and underparts* • black wingtips and tail • white on upperparts of secondaries.

### ADULT FEMALE

Similar to adult male except for • darker gray head • whitish mottling on undertail coverts • dark gray tail with black terminal band.

### SECOND YEAR

Similar to adult except for • dark gray on upperparts of secondaries • thin white bands in tail.

### FLEDGLING TO FIRST SPRING

Similar to second year except for • thin dark streaks on head • white edges to

**Fledgling to first spring** WHEELER

Adult male                                    WHEELER

Fledgling to first spring                      WHEELER

feathers of upperparts • *thick rufous streaks on underparts.*

## FLIGHT TRAITS

Pointed wings • *overall shape falconlike* • *graceful flight.*

## ADULT MALE

*Pale gray head • gray underparts • white secondaries and rufous parts in primaries seen on upperwing • thin, white trailing edge on wings • black tail.*

## ADULT FEMALE

Similar to adult male except for • darker gray head • whitish mottling on undertail coverts • tail dark gray with a black terminal band.

## SECOND YEAR

Similar to adult except for • dark gray secondaries and no rufous parts in primaries on upperwing • variable rufous mottling on wing linings (becomes more gray by the late part of the summer) • thin white bands in tail.

## FLEDGLING TO FIRST SPRING

Similar to second year except for • *thick*

*rufous streaks on underparts* • *thick rufous mottling on wing linings.*

## LISTEN FOR

A high whistle *fee-teeew.*

## COMPARE TO

Peregrine Falcon, Merlin.

## RANGE

■ Breeding only
■ Wintering only

31

# *Haliaeetus leucocephalus*

Adult

SMALL

I'M SURE ALMOST EVERYONE reading this can remember their first good look at a Bald Eagle. And if you haven't seen one yet, you will be impressed when you do. This is the largest raptor in eastern North America and, though they share the name "eagle," it is not very closely related to the Golden Eagle (pages 72–73). After a drastic decline in numbers due to shootings and the effects of pesticides, Bald Eagles are recovering and now breed in every province and state except Vermont and Rhode Island.

## SIZE

Length much > Red-tailed Hawk
Wingspan > Great Blue Heron

## ADULT

*Large, all white head • yellow beak • yellow eyes • all dark brown body • all white tail and white undertail coverts.*

Note: Figuring out the age of immature Bald Eagles is tricky due to individual variation.

## THIRD & FOURTH YEAR

All dark brown with some white mottling on belly and back • pale yellow eyes • whitish head with dark mottling (may have a thick dark eyeline) • yellow beak (may have dusky patches or tip) • whitish tail with dark terminal band. (Fourth year can be very close to adult plumage.)

First year

WHEELER

Adult

SMALL

## SECOND YEAR

Similar to third and fourth year birds except for • darker head with less distinctive eyeline • grayish beak with dark tip • usually brown eyes.

## FIRST YEAR

Similar to second year bird except for • dark brown head • less whitish mottling • buffy, light brown or dark brown belly • dark eyes.

## FLIGHT TRAITS

Very long, wide wings • wings held flat or at a slight dihedral or "V" • large head • flaps with fairly stiff, slow wing beats.

## ADULT

*White head* • brown body and wings • *white tail and undertail coverts*.

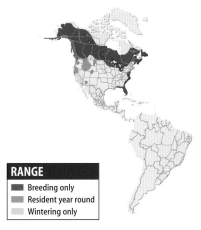

### RANGE
■ Breeding only
■ Resident year round
■ Wintering only

Third year SMALL

### THIRD & FOURTH YEAR

Whitish head with dark mottling (may have a thick, dark eyeline) • whitish tail with dark terminal band • *variable amounts of white mottling on belly, wing linings and secondaries.* (Fourth year can be very close to adult plumage.)

### SECOND YEAR

Similar to third and fourth year except for • browner head • possibly more *white mottling on belly, wing linings and secondaries* • jagged trailing edge on wings (some feathers longer than others).

### FIRST YEAR

Similar to second year except for • dark brown head • buffy, light brown or dark brown on belly • may have a darker tail • no jagged trailing edge on wings.

### LISTEN FOR

Call described by Bent (1937) as "ridiculously weak and insignificant." A fast, chattering series of notes *ki-ki-kir-ker-ker-kur-kur.*

### COMPARE TO

Golden Eagle, Turkey Vulture, Osprey.

### NATURE NOTES

The oldest recorded age for a Bald Eagle in the wild is 28 years.

Second year WHEELER

First year

Second year

Third year

## *Circus cyaneus*

**Adult male**

**First year male**

ONCE CALLED THE MARSH HAWK, the Northern Harrier is the only harrier found in North America. They have a distinctive hunting style that is well described by Thoreau (1856): "the marsh hawks flew in their usual irregular low tacking, wheeling, and circling flight, leisurely flapping and beating, now rising, now falling, in conformity with the contour of the ground." This is the only North American hawk that has facial disks, allowing it to locate prey by sound like owls can. So, by staying close to the ground, they are able to watch *and* listen effectively for prey.

Adult male in flight

WHEELER

## SIZE

Length:   male = American Crow
          female = Red-tailed Hawk
Wingspan: male = American Crow
          female < Red-tailed Hawk

### ADULT MALE

*Smoky gray head and back* • *facial disks*
• yellow eyes • whitish belly with rufous
spots • dark wingtips • *white rump* (hard
to see on perched birds) • long, gray tail
with dark bands • long legs.

### ADULT FEMALE

Brown head and back • *facial disks*
• yellow eyes • buffy underparts with dark
streaks • *white rump* (hard to see on
perched birds) • long, brown tail with
dark bands • long legs.

### RANGE
■ Breeding only
■ Resident year round
  Wintering only

Adult female on nest

## FIRST YEAR

Similar to adult female except for
• unstreaked (or a few streaks), *orange-rufous breast and belly* (can fade considerably by spring) • pale eyes on males, dark brown eyes on females.

### FLIGHT TRAITS

*Wings held in a strong dihedral or "V"*
• leading edge of wings pushed forward when soaring • long wings and tail • *often flies close to the ground* • rocks or teeters like a Turkey Vulture.

## ADULT MALE

Smoky gray head and upper breast
• *white belly, undertail coverts and underwings* • some rufous spots on belly and wing linings • *black wingtips* (like a gull) • black trailing edge to secondaries

First year male

• whitish tail with dusky bands • *white rump when viewed from above.*

## ADULT FEMALE

Brown head • buffy underparts and wing linings with dark streaks • darkish patch on wing linings close to the body

Adult female

First year female showing white rump

• banded primaries, secondaries and tail feathers • *white rump when seen from above.*

## ⚡ FIRST YEAR

Similar to the adult female except for
• unstreaked (or a few streaks), *orange-*

*rufous breast, belly and wing linings* (can fade considerably by spring).

### LISTEN FOR

A high *kek-kek-kek-kek-kek-kek*.

### COMPARE TO

Cooper's Hawk, Northern Goshawk, Peregrine Falcon.

### NATURE NOTES

The color differences between adult males and females of this species are the most pronounced of all the birds in this book (except for the American Kestrel, pages 74–77). The male's coloration is very similar to a gull's; both have smoky gray upperparts, white underparts and black wingtips. Northern Harriers nest on the ground and so are vulnerable to predators such as coyotes, foxes and skunks.

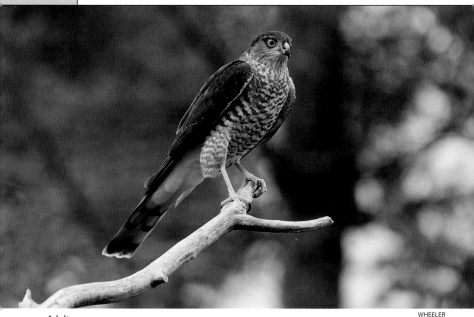

**Adult**

LITTLE BIRDS BEWARE! THE Sharp-shinned Hawk is certainly a predator that needs to be watched for. They catch their avian prey through fast, surprise attacks, as described by Studer (1881): "Its flight is peculiar – swift, spirited, and irregular, now soaring high into the air, then suddenly sweeping close to the ground. It seems to advance by sudden dashes, and when once its prey is discovered, will pounce upon it with a swiftness which makes escape impossible." Winter bird feeders often become real "bird feeders" when a local sharpie zips in and catches a junco or

**First year**

goldfinch. But because of their small size, these hawks have to be careful, too, or they will end up on the menu of other raptors, such as Peregrine Falcons.

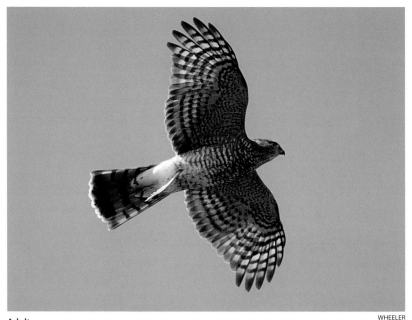

Adult

## SIZE

| | |
|---|---|
| Length: | male = American Robin |
| | female = Rock Pigeon |
| Wingspan: | male > Mourning Dove |
| | female = Killdeer |

## ADULT

Small head • red eyes • bluish gray back, wings and tail (female may be a brownish gray above) • *thick, rusty-orange barring on white breast and belly* • may have orange on cheeks • white undertail coverts • may have a few white spots on back • thick, dark bands on tail • *squarish tail* with thin, white terminal band (note that from below, the outer tail feathers are the same or not much shorter than others) • long, thin legs.

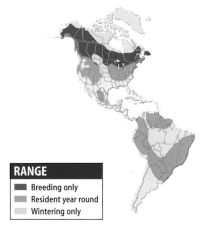

**RANGE**

- Breeding only
- Resident year round
- Wintering only

**41**

Adult with red eyes                    FLYNN

First year with yellow eyes            McCAW

Adult                                  SMALL

## FIRST YEAR

Similar to the adult except for • yellow eyes • brown back and wings (may have some small whitish patches) • brownish gray tail • *thick brown streaks on white breast and belly*.

## FLIGHT TRAITS

Wings usually held flat when soaring • *small head* • rounded wings • flapping of wings is floppy, not stiff • leading edge of wings often pushed forward when soaring • *long tail with squarish tip* • *often flies with the typical accipiter pattern of a group of flaps and then a glide*.

## ADULT

Red eyes • bluish gray back, wings and tail • thick, rusty-orange barring on white breast, belly and wing linings • white undertail coverts • dark bands on primaries, secondaries and tail feathers • banded tail with thin white terminal band.

First year

WHEELER

## 🔪 FIRST YEAR

Similar to adult in flight except for • *thick, brown streaks* on white breast and belly • brown streaks on white wing linings • bands on primaries and secondaries not as distinct.

## LISTEN FOR

A high *kek-kek-kek-kek-kek-kek*.

## COMPARE TO

Cooper's Hawk (see comparison pages 118–21), American Kestrel, Mourning Dove.

## NATURE NOTES

Sharp-shinned Hawks take prey as small as hummingbirds and as large as Ruffed Grouse, but focus on birds the size of warblers, sparrows and thrushes. Usually less than 10 percent of their diet is small mammals and insects.

THE MID-SIZE MODEL OF OUR three accipiters, the wings and tail of a Cooper's Hawk are proportionally longer than the others. While this can be a good identification clue for experienced birders, it will take beginners a while before these shape characteristics become useful. Cooper's Hawks focus on larger prey than the Sharp-shinned; these include robins, jays, flickers, starlings and chipmunks. Even larger prey include pheasants, quail, doves, crows and gray squirrels. Another favorite, the Rock Dove or pigeon, is often hunted right above busy city streets. The next time you are walking through town and see a large, closely packed flock of pigeons flying rapidly and being reluctant to land, take a minute and see if the reason for their uneasiness is a dashing Cooper's Hawk.

Adult      FLYNN

First year      WHEELER

### SIZE

Length:    male < American Crow
            female = American Crow
Wingspan:   male = Rock Pigeon
            female > Rock Pigeon

### ADULT

Red eyes • bluish gray back, wings and tail (female may be brownish gray above) • *thick, rusty-orange barring on white breast and belly* • may have a dark crown

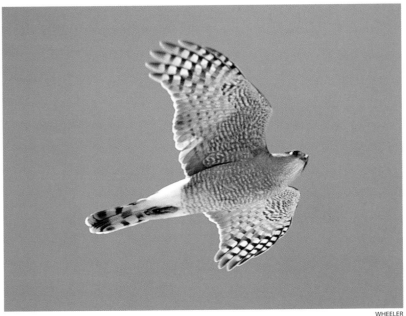

**Adult**

WHEELER

• white undertail coverts • thick, dark bands on tail • *rounded tail with a fairly thick white terminal band* (note that from beneath, the outer tail feathers are much shorter than the others) • long, strong-looking legs.

### FIRST YEAR

Similar to perched adult except for • yellow eyes • brown back and wings (may have some small whitish patches) • *thin brown streaks on white breast and belly* • white undertail coverts with no streaking • brownish gray tail.

### FLIGHT TRAITS

Wings usually held flat when soaring • rounded wings • *proportionally longer wings and tail than other accipiters* • large head • straight leading edge on wings when soaring • *wings quite stiff when*

*flapping* • long tail is rounded at the tip • *often flies with the typical accipiter pattern of a group of flaps and then a glide.*

**RANGE**
■ Breeding only
■ Resident year round
■ Wintering only

Adult                                                    WHEELER

### ADULT

*Thick, rusty-orange barring on white breast, belly and wing linings* • white undertail coverts • dark bands on primaries, secondaries and tail feathers • banded tail with fairly thick white terminal band.

### FIRST YEAR

Similar to adult in flight except for • narrow brown streaks on white breast and belly • brown streaks on white wing linings • bands on primaries and secondaries not as distinct.

### LISTEN FOR

A loud alarm call of *kak-kak-kak-kak-kak-kak*.

### COMPARE TO

Sharp-shinned Hawk, Northern Goshawk (see comparison pages, 118–21).

### NATURE NOTES

It is thought that one of the main food items for this species was once the now extinct Passenger Pigeon.

This shows the extreme size difference between male and female accipiters.

WHEELER

First year

WHEELER

## *Accipiter gentilis*

**Adult**                                               FLYNN

**First year**                                          LYNCH

"BEAUTY AND COURAGE, SWIFTNESS and strength mean something to us; and we shall find these qualities in high degree in the hawks of the Accipiter clan. Especially is this true of the largest and strongest of them, the goshawk, one of the deadliest, handsomest, bravest birds of prey in the world," wrote Sass (1930, in Bent). If you've ever been near a Northern Goshawk's active nest, then this quote probably hits home. And "hitting home" is exactly what the parents will try to do if you are close to their nest. Their loud "*kak, kak, kak, kak, kak*" alarm call gives you a short warning that ducking your head might be a good idea. Just thinking about it makes my spine tingle. The Northern Goshawk is our largest accipiter and it focuses on prey such as hares, squirrels, grouse, woodpeckers, jays, crows and smaller birds. I used to watch one hunt on a farm that had a bird feeder on one side of the farmhouse and a driveway on the other. The goshawk would fly rapidly and low up the driveway, then swoop around one end of the house and suddenly appear at the feeder, much to the dismay of the local Mourning Doves.

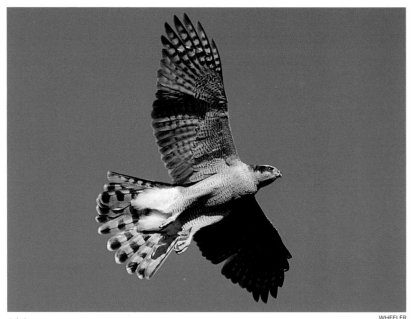

Adult

WHEELER

## SIZE

Length:　male = Red-tailed Hawk
　　　　　female > Red-tailed Hawk
Wingspan:　male = American Crow
　　　　　female > American Crow

### 🗡 ADULT

Dark crown and eyeline • *thick white eyebrow* • red eyes • bluish gray back, wings and tail • *very thin, gray barring on white breast and belly* (can be thicker on females) • white undertail coverts • strong-looking legs.

### 🗡 FIRST YEAR

Similar to perched adult except for • yellow eyes • thinner eyebrow and no eyeline • brown back and wings (may have some small whitish patches) • *thick brown streaks on buffy or whitish breast*

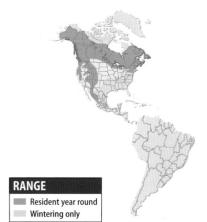

### RANGE
■ Resident year round
■ Wintering only

49

First year

WHEELER

*and belly* • some streaks on white undertail coverts • brownish gray tail with dark, thick, jagged bands • each tail band has a thin, light border on upper surface.

## FLIGHT TRAITS

Rounded wings *but often have a tapered or pointed appearance* • *most buteolike accipiter* • large head • straight leading edge on wings when soaring • flaps deeply, like a buteo • long, broad tail • *often flies with the typical accipiter pattern of a group of flaps and then a glide.*

## ADULT

*Very thin, gray barring on white breast, belly and wing linings* (can be thicker on females) • white undertail coverts • dark bands on primaries • upperwing has dark primaries and secondaries with the rest of the wing lighter gray.

## FIRST YEAR

Similar to adult in flight except for • *thick brown streaks on buffy or white breast and belly* • *some brown streaks on undertail coverts* • brown streaks on white wing linings • bands on primaries and secondaries • bands on tail appear jagged, especially from above • each tail band has a thin, light border (if you are close enough to see it) • pale light bar on upperwing.

## LISTEN FOR

A loud alarm call of *kak-kak-kak-kak-kak-kak*.

## COMPARE TO

Cooper's Hawk (see comparison pages, 118–21), Red-shouldered Hawk, Red-tailed Hawk, Gyrfalcon.

## NATURE NOTES

Northern Goshawks have been known to kill other raptor species such as Sharp-shinned Hawks, Long-eared Owls, Red-tailed Hawks and even other goshawks.

First year

First year

## *Buteo lineatus*

Adult

THIS BUTEO PREFERS WET FORESTS and wooded river valleys. Here it often hunts from a perch, watching for frogs, small mammals, snakes, small birds, insects, fish, earthworms and crayfish. In other words, the Red-shouldered Hawk isn't too choosy. It used to be much more common in the Great Lakes region, but habitat degradation has caused its numbers to decline here.

### SIZE

Length = American Crow
Wingspan = American Crow

### ADULT

Brown head and back with some whitish mottling • *blackish primaries, secondaries and tail feathers with thin white bands* • *reddish shoulders* (not always apparent) • thick, rusty-orange barring on white breast and belly • white undertail coverts • short tail (note: birds in Florida are much paler overall).

### FIRST YEAR

Similar to adult except for • brown primaries, secondaries and tail feathers with dark bands • thick brown streaks on white breast and belly.

### FLIGHT TRAITS

Wide, rounded wings • stiff wing beats • wings held flat or droop slightly when soaring • broad tail.

First year

Adult – note "window" on lower wing due to lighting conditions    WHEELER

First year – note "windows" on both wings    WHEELER

## ADULT

*Rusty-orange barring on white breast and belly* • *rusty-orange wing linings* (may be paler than breast and belly) • thin black bands on primaries and secondaries • dark tips on primaries • *translucent "window" near tips of primaries* (note: other hawks may have "windows" in their wings while they are molting; these are different than the "windows" of a Red-shouldered, but can be confusing for beginning birders) • thick black trailing edge on secondaries • white undertail coverts • *black tail with two or three thin white bands visible plus a thin white terminal band.*

## FIRST YEAR

Similar to adult except for • thick dark streaks on white breast and belly • white wing linings • indistinct bands on primaries and secondaries • indistinct dark trailing edge on secondaries • dark tips on primaries • tail with many dark bands.

## LISTEN FOR

A loud, screamed *keeyaah*.

## COMPARE TO

Broad-winged Hawk, Red-tailed Hawk, Northern Goshawk.

## NATURE NOTES

The Red-shouldered Hawk has an elaborate and noisy courtship display flight that includes fast dives and climbs while giving loud screams.

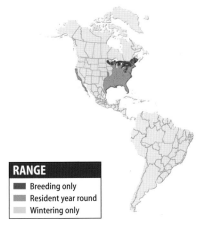

### RANGE

- Breeding only
- Resident year round
- Wintering only

OUR SMALLEST BUTEO, THE Broad-winged Hawk is another raptor who opts for a wide variety of prey. They eat small mammals, young birds, insects and seem to have a liking for frogs and toads as well. Brewster (1925, in Bent), wrote, "After alighting on a low branch or stub overlooking some shallow reach of calm water besprinkled with innumerable floating toads absorbed in the cares and pleasures of procreation, and rending the still air with the ceaseless din of their tremulous voices, the Hawk will often gaze down at them long and listlessly, as if undecided which particular one to select from among so many, or dreamily gloat over the wealth of opportunities for such selection."

**Adult light morph**      WHEELER

### SIZE

Length < American Crow
Wingspan < American Crow

### ❚ ADULT

Brown head and back • no distinct bands on primaries and secondaries • thick, rusty-orange barring on white breast and belly • white undertail coverts • *short tail with thick white band.*

**First year**      WHEELER

Adult light morph

WHEELER

## FIRST YEAR

Similar to perched adult except for • thick dark streaks on white breast and belly • short tail with one dark, thick subterminal band and many thin bands.

## FLIGHT TRAITS

Wings held flat when soaring • slightly pointed, wide wings • stiff wing beats • fairly short tail.

## ADULT

*Rusty barring on white breast and belly • white wing linings with a few rusty bars • black primary tips • thick, black trailing edge on wings • tail has a thin, white terminal band, then two thick black bands separated by one thick white band.*

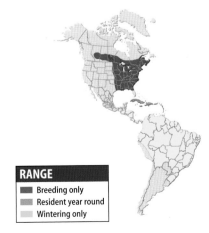

**RANGE**
- Breeding only
- Resident year round
- Wintering only

First year dark morph                    WHEELER

Adult dark morph                    WHEELER

## FIRST YEAR

Similar to adult in flight except for • dark streaks on white breast and belly • white wing linings with variable dark streaks • dusky primary tips • thick, dusky trailing edge on wings • tail has a white terminal band, a fairly thick, dark subterminal band and many thin, dark bands.

## DARK MORPH

The dark Broad-winged Hawk is a rare western-range morph. It is very rarely seen in the east during migration. This morph has primaries, secondaries and *tail feathers* similar to the light morph, but the body and the wing linings are very dark brown to black.

## LISTEN FOR

A high, thin, two-parted whistle with the second part slightly lower than the first. A *peeyurr*.

## COMPARE TO

Red-shouldered Hawk, Red-tailed Hawk.

## NATURE NOTES

The Broad-winged Hawk gives us one of the most spectacular migration displays in the animal kingdom. Hundreds of these hawks may circle together in a flock or "kettle" as they use uprisings of warm air called thermals to stay aloft. On September 17, 1999, in the Lake Erie Metropark, the Southern Michigan Raptor Research group counted an amazing 555,371 Broad-winged Hawks migrating southwards.

Migrating Broad-winged Hawks in a "kettle"

WHEELER

First year

WHEELER

# *Buteo swainsoni*

**Adult light morph**

**First year light morph**

ANOTHER BUTEO THAT MIGRATES in large flocks, the Swainson's Hawk is a prairie bird of the west that is sometimes found in the Great Lakes region during migration. It winters in central and southern South America – a distance of over 6,250 miles (10,000 km) from its breeding range in Canada. This means it travels over 12,500 miles (20,000 km) round-trip each year. Unfortunately, they are in much danger while in many parts of their winter range where thousands die every year because of pesticide poisoning.

Adult light morph

## SIZE

Length = Red-tailed Hawk
Wingspan = Red-tailed Hawk

## LIGHT MORPH ADULT

Dark head with white forehead and throat · *white underparts with solid rufous breast* · dark brown back and wings · short tail with thick, dark subterminal band and many thinner bands.

## LIGHT MORPH FIRST & SECOND YEAR

Buffy or whitish head (especially on early spring birds) · dark brown back and wings with white mottling · whitish underparts with dark streaks (*often forming a dark patch on the sides of the breast*) · tail with many thin, dark bands.

### RANGE

■ Breeding only
■ Wintering only

Adult intermediate morph                    WHEELER

Adult dark morph                    WHEELER

First year dark morph                    WHEELER

## FLIGHT TRAITS

Wings held in a dihedral or "V" when soaring • rocks or teeters like a Turkey Vulture or Northern Harrier • long, wide wings that are quite pointed for a buteo • relatively long, broad tail.

## ◣ LIGHT MORPH ADULT

White throat • *white underparts with a solid rufous breast* • *white wing linings contrasting with the dark primaries and secondaries* • finely barred tail with a thick, dark subterminal band.

## ◤◣ INTERMEDIATE MORPH ADULT

Similar to light morph adult except for • dark brown breast • rufous belly • rufous in wing linings.

Adult intermediate morph

WHEELER

Adult dark morph

WHEELER

### DARK MORPH ADULT

Similar to intermediate morph adult except for • no white throat • dark brown to black breast and belly • white undertail coverts (may have dark marks) • rufous or dark markings on wing linings.

### LIGHT MORPH FIRST YEAR

Similar to light morph adult in flight except for • *solid patches on sides of breast only* • dark streaks on breast and belly • dark streaks on wing linings • primaries, secondaries and tail feathers not as dark • less distinct thick subterminal band on tail. (Second year birds similar except with mostly adult primaries, secondaries and tail feathers.)

### INTERMEDIATE & DARK MORPH FIRST YEARS

Similar to light morph first year except for • dark mottling on breast and belly • dark mottling in wing linings.

### LISTEN FOR

A shrill, screaming whistle *kweeeeeeee*.

### COMPARE TO

Dark morph to dark morph Rough-legged Hawk and Harlan's Red-tailed Hawk.

### NATURE NOTES

These hawks can be fierce defenders of their nests. As a young, budding 17-year-old naturalist, I was excited to find a Swainson's Hawk nest on my uncle's farm in southern Saskatchewan. While looking up at the chicks, a rushing sound preceded one of the parent's knocking my cap off. As it dove again and again, I ran terrified to my motorcycle and took off. That didn't deter the bird at all, and it almost succeeded in knocking me off the racing motorcycle!

**Adult Eastern** McCAW

**First year Eastern** SMALL

THE RED-TAILED HAWK IS LIKELY the best known raptor in this book and one of the easiest of our raptors to identify – at least the adults are. Try not to focus too much on the red tail for identification purposes, though. Learn other field marks and behaviors so you will have a better "comparison hawk" when looking at other species. The relative abundance of Red-tailed Hawks also allows birders to observe much of their breeding biology, from courtship to nest building to raising their young.

## SIZE

Length > American Crow
Wingspan much > American Crow

### EASTERN ADULT

Brown head • dark eyes • white throat • brown back and wings • *light marks on wings form a "V" that can be seen from quite a distance* • whitish or buffy underparts with variable amounts of dark streaks on belly (*often forming a belly band*) • *short, red tail*.

### EASTERN FIRST YEAR

Similar to adult perched except for • yellow eyes • whiter underparts with more dark streaking • *brown tail with many thin bands*.

### FLIGHT TRAITS

Wings held in a very shallow dihedral or "V" when soaring • wide, long, rounded wings • fluid wing beats • broad tail.

Adult Eastern (a fairly pale individual – the photo at the bottom right of page 65 is more typical for this area)

WHEELER

## 🦅 EASTERN ADULT

Whitish or buffy underparts with variable amounts of dark streaks on belly (*often forming a belly band*) • white or buffy wing linings • *dark patagial mark* • *dark "commas" on wrists* • dark tipped primaries • dark trailing edge to secondaries • banded primaries and secondaries • *short, red tail.*

## 🦅 EASTERN FIRST YEAR

Similar to adult in flight except for
• yellow eyes • whiter underparts with more dark streaking • *upperwing has light brown outer half and darker brown inner half* • *tail is brown with many thin bands.*

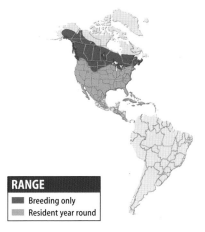

| RANGE | |
|---|---|
| ■ | Breeding only |
| ■ | Resident year round |

# Red-tailed Hawk

Adult Eastern

McCAW

## MORPHS

There is a lot of variation in the Red-tailed Hawk across North America, especially in the west. Many look similar to our eastern birds, but there are some dark and intermediate morphs. Still others are quite a bit paler than the eastern birds. For identification purposes of flying birds, all Red-tailed Hawks have *dark patagial marks* (except for dark morphs, where the wing linings are all dark). As well, all juvenile Red-tailed Hawks have narrow bands on their tails. All adults have a *red or reddish tail*, except for one, the Harlan's Red-tail, which has a whitish to gray tail that blends to a darker gray on the tip. Check out the photos to see some of these variations, but keep in mind that they are all rare in the Great Lakes region.

## LISTEN FOR

A rough, screamed descending whistle *keeee-arrrrrrr.*

## COMPARE TO

Rough-legged Hawk, Ferruginous Hawk.

## NATURE NOTES

Partial albinism seems to occur more frequently in Red-tailed Hawks than in other raptor species. These birds may have white feathers in patches or covering most of the body.

**First year Eastern**                    WHEELER

**First year Eastern**                    WHEELER

**Adult Harlan's**                        WHEELER

**Adult dark morph**                      WHEELER

**Adult Eastern**                         McCAW

## Buteo regalis

**Adult light morph and adult dark morph**

McCAW

THIS PRAIRIE BUTEO IS SO ROBUST that some think it should be called an eagle. Its head and beak shape look surprisingly eaglelike as well. It is a very rare visitor to most of the Great Lakes region during migration, but is regular in Minnesota.

### SIZE

Length > Red-tailed Hawk
Wingspan > Red-tailed Hawk

### 🐦 LIGHT MORPH ADULT

Large head and beak • grayish head with white throat • rufous back and wings with gray primaries and secondaries • *white underparts with some rufous barring on belly sides and leg feathers • whitish or light rufous tail.*

### 🐦 LIGHT MORPH FIRST YEAR

Similar to adult except for • yellow eyes • brown back and wings • some dark streaking on belly and legs, no rufous • brownish tail with a few narrow bars.

Adult light morph     WHEELER

Adult dark morph     WHEELER

## FLIGHT TRAITS

The most eaglelike buteo • large head • wings held in a dihedral or "V" when soaring • long, wide, rounded wings • flaps with fluid wing beats • long, broad tail.

## LIGHT MORPH ADULT

*White underparts • rufous leg feathers • whitish or light rufous tail* • white wings with some rufous barring on wing linings • dark wing tips • the base of the primaries on the upperwing forms a light patch.

## LIGHT MORPH FIRST YEAR

Similar to adult in flight except for • no rufous on leg feathers • no rufous on wing linings, dark spots instead • faint narrow bars on tail.

## DARK MORPH

All dark brown body and wing linings • *narrow white comma near wrist in flight* • white primaries, secondaries and tail feathers with some very faint barring.

## LISTEN FOR

A weak, low whistle *keeeer.*

## COMPARE TO

Rough-legged Hawk, Red-tailed Hawk.

## NATURE NOTES

When bison still roamed the prairies, their bones were often used as part of the Ferruginous Hawk's nesting material.

### RANGE

■ Breeding only
■ Resident year round
■ Wintering only

**Adult male light morph** WHEELER

A WINTER VISITOR TO THIS AREA, the Rough-legged Hawk is a strikingly handsome buteo. Bent (1937) wrote, "the mention of its name brings visions of a splendid bird, one of the largest and finest of our hawks. Past master in the use of air currents, whether it is posed motionless in a breeze over a cliff, or scaling close to the ground and quartering like a harrier, or swinging proudly in great circles up and up into the blue sky, this great hawk is always a thing of beauty." The sun's reflections on a field of newly fallen snow often light up the undersides of flying Rough-legs, making their markings even more appealing. The dark morph of this hawk is the only commonly seen dark morph hawk in the Great Lakes region.

**First year light morph** WHEELER

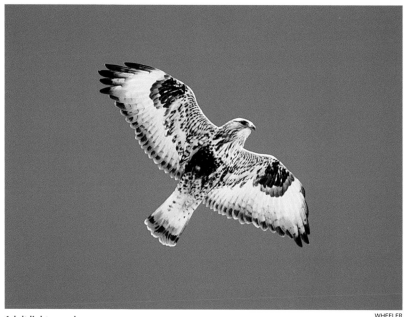

Adult light morph

WHEELER

## SIZE

Length > Red-tailed Hawk
Wingspan > Red-tailed Hawk

## LIGHT MORPH ADULT MALE

Pale head • dark eyes • dark upper breast with white mottling • *white lower breast and belly with dark mottling* • white undertail coverts • dark back with white mottling • *light tail with white terminal band, thick, dark subterminal band and one or two narrow, dark bands.* (Note: there is a lot of variation between males and females, so not all birds can be sexed by plumage.)

## LIGHT MORPH ADULT FEMALE

Similar to the light morph adult male except for • light upper breast with dark streaks • *more solidly dark belly band*

*• whitish tail with white terminal band, thick, dark subterminal band and a thick, dusky band.*

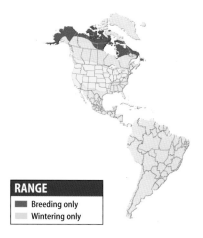

### RANGE

■ Breeding only
░ Wintering only

Adult male dark morph     WHEELER

Adult female light morph     WHEELER

## LIGHT MORPH FIRST YEAR

Similar to light morph adult female except for • light eyes • only the thick, dusky subterminal band on tail.

## DARK MORPH

Very dark brown head, wing linings and body (male may be black overall) • dark eyes (first year has light eyes) • *light tail with white terminal band, thick, dark subterminal band and zero to three narrow, dark bands.*

## FLIGHT TRAITS

*Wings held in a dihedral or "V," though the outer parts of the wings are quite horizontal* • long, wide, rounded wings • flaps with fluid wing beats • relatively long, broad tail.

## LIGHT MORPH ADULT MALE

Pale head • dark eyes • dark upper breast with white mottling • *white lower breast and belly with dark mottling* • white undertail coverts • light wing linings with dark mottling • *dark wrist patch* • dark tips to primaries and secondaries • some light banding in secondaries • *light tail with white terminal band, thick, dark subterminal band and one or two narrow, dark bands.* (There is a lot of variation between males and females, so not all birds can be sexed by plumage.)

## LIGHT MORPH ADULT FEMALE

Similar to the light morph adult male except for • light upper breast with dark streaks • *more solidly dark belly band* • brown mottling in wing linings • *darker wrist patches* • *whitish tail with white*

Adult dark morph
WHEELER

First year dark morph
WHEELER

*terminal band, thick, dark subterminal band and a thick, dusky band.*

## LIGHT MORPH FIRST YEAR

Similar to light morph female except for
• light eyes • less defined dark tips to
secondaries • less brown in wing linings
• only the thick, dusky subterminal band
on tail.

## DARK MORPH

Very dark brown head, wing linings and
body (male may be black overall) • dark
eyes (first year has light eyes) • white
primaries and secondaries • dark tips on
primaries • *dark wrist patches show on
brown individuals* • dark banding in
secondaries • *light tail with white terminal
band, thick, dark subterminal band and
zero to three narrow, dark bands.*

First year light morph
WHEELER

## NATURE NOTES

Compared to other buteos of similar size,
the Rough-legged Hawk has proportionally
smaller feet and beak. This relates to its
preference for smaller prey, though it
does take larger prey occasionally.

## LISTEN FOR

A thin whistled *keeeyurrrrr.*

## COMPARE TO

Ferruginous Hawk, Red-tailed Hawk,
Osprey.

# *Aquila chrysaetos*

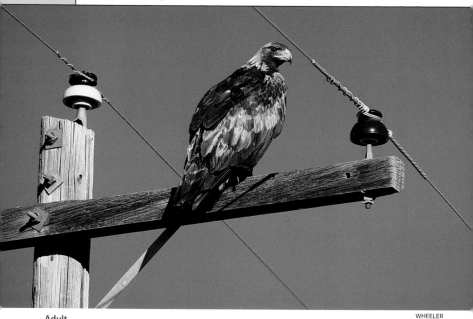

Adult

"THIS MAGNIFICENT EAGLE HAS long been named the King of Birds and it well deserves the title. It is majestic in flight, regal in appearance, dignified in manner and crowned with a shower of golden hackles about its royal head," (Bent, 1937). It's hard to think of many birds more awe-inspiring than the Golden Eagle. A formidable predator, there are even records of these eagles working together and attacking full-grown pronghorn antelope and deer! But very large prey are rarely taken and the Golden Eagle's regular diet includes hares, marmots and carrion.

## SIZE

Length = Bald Eagle
Wingspan > Great Blue Heron

## ADULT

Dark brown head, body and wings • *tawny nape and eyebrow* • tawny-brown undertail coverts • dark tail with narrow lighter bands.

## FIRST & UP TO FIFTH YEAR

Similar to adult except for • second to fifth years have variable whitish mottled base to tail • *first year has all white base to tail, leaving a thick, dark terminal band.*

## FLIGHT TRAITS

Wings held flat or in a shallow dihedral or "V" • *relatively small head* • long, wide, rounded wings • flaps with slow, fluid wing beats.

Adult
WHEELER

First year
WHEELER

## ADULT

Dark brown head, wing linings and body • tawny nape and eyebrow • tawny-brown undertail coverts • dark primaries, secondaries and tail feathers with faint banding.

## FIRST & UP TO FIFTH YEAR

Similar to adult except for • second to fifth years have variable whitish mottled base on tail and may have some white bases to outer secondaries and inner primaries • *first year has all white base to tail, leaving a thick, dark terminal band* • *first year usually shows white patch at the base of the outer secondaries and inner primaries.*

## LISTEN FOR

Shrill yelps.

## COMPARE TO

Immature Bald Eagle, Turkey Vulture.

"Mantling" over its kill
LYNCH

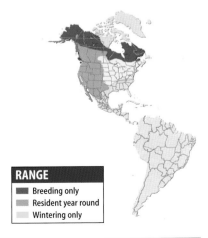

| RANGE | |
|---|---|
| ■ | Breeding only |
| ■ | Resident year round |
| ■ | Wintering only |

## *Falco sparverius*

Adult male FLYNN

Adult female SMALL

THIS IS THE SMALLEST OF OUR falcons and though it is less powerful than the others, it makes up for this by being the most colorful hawk in the world. It also has a special hunting style that is not frequently used by other hawks. Winsor Marrett Tyler wrote, "Perhaps the most remarkable of its aerial accomplishments, the bird, arresting its flight through the air, hovers, facing the wind, its body tilted upward to a slight angle with the ground, its wings beating lightly and easily." From its held position, the kestrel is able to drop onto an unsuspecting meadow vole or grasshopper. It also hunts from perches and is often seen sitting on telephone wires where it may be mistaken for a Mourning Dove.

### SIZE

Length = American Robin
Wingspan < Killdeer

### ADULT MALE

Bluish gray cap with rufous central spot • *white face with thick black mustache and sideburns* • two large black spots on back of head • *rufous back with dark barring on lower back* • *bluish gray wings with dark spots* • pale rufous breast blending to whiter undertail coverts • dark spots on belly • *long, narrow, bright rufous tail*

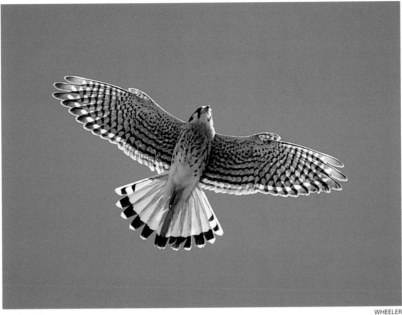

Adult male

• *white outer tail feathers, which may have dark spots* • *tail has thin, white terminal band and thick, black subterminal band* • *often pumps its tail.*

### ADULT FEMALE

Similar to adult male except for • more subdued head pattern with gray cap • white underparts with rufous streaks on breast and belly • wings rufous with dark barring • *tail rufous with narrow dark bands* (subterminal band thicker than others).

### FIRST YEAR MALE

Similar to adult male except for • more dark barring on back • thin dark breast and belly streaks (first year females very similar to adult females).

### FLIGHT TRAITS

Long, pointed wings • wings held flat • *long, narrow tail* • *not a strong-looking flyer* like the other falcons • *often hovers.*

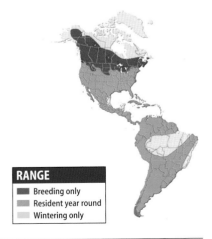

### RANGE
- Breeding only
- Resident year round
- Wintering only

Male Kestrel with a baby turtle it has just caught

McCAW

### ADULT MALE

White throat and black mustache • *pale rufous breast blending to whiter undertail coverts* • dark spots on belly • pale rufous wing linings with black spots • primaries and secondaries with many thin, dark bands • *long, bright rufous tail with thin, white terminal band and thick, black subterminal band* • white outer tail feathers with variable amounts of dark spots.

### ADULT FEMALE

Similar to adult male except for • white underparts with rufous streaks on breast and belly • light wing linings with light rufous spots • *long tail rufous with narrow dark bands* (subterminal one thicker than others).

### FIRST YEAR MALE

Similar to adult male except for • thin dark breast and belly streaks (first year females very similar to adult females).

### LISTEN FOR

A loud *killy-killy-killy-killy-killy*.

### COMPARE TO

Merlin, Sharp-shinned Hawk, Mourning Dove.

### NATURE NOTES

The American Kestrel often nests in old woodpecker holes and will also use nest boxes (see page 111). Because kestrels can see ultraviolet light, and because vole urine reflects that color, it's possible that kestrels can follow vole urine trails to potential prey.

Adult female

WHEELER

Adult female at nest cavity in abandoned ranch building

WHEELER

# *Falco columbarius*

**Adult male**

**First year female**

THE MERLIN MAY BE LITTLE, BUT to small birds it is an unforgiving predator. Merlins often hunt by perching near an open field or lake and waiting for a small bird to cross. Then the falcon just flies down its meal with an impressive burst of speed. They also catch flying insects such as dragonflies, as well as bats that are leaving their daytime cave roosts.

## SIZE

Length = American Robin
Wingspan = Killdeer

Adult male

WHEELER

Note the thin white bands in the tail

SMALL

### ADULT MALE

Bluish gray head and upperparts • dusky, indistinct mustache • pale rufous to whitish underparts with dark streaks • *black tail with light narrow bands.*

### ADULT FEMALE & FIRST YEAR

Similar to male except for • whiter underparts with dark streaks • brown upperparts.

### FLIGHT TRAITS

*A very strong flyer* • relatively short, pointed wings.

### ADULT MALE

Dusky, indistinct mustache • whitish throat • pale rufous to whitish underparts with dark streaks • dark underwings with white spotting • *black tail with narrow white bands.*

### ADULT FEMALE & FIRST YEAR

Similar to adult male except for • whiter underparts with dark streaks.

### WESTERN MERLINS

Merlins in the prairies are lighter overall and those on the west coast can be very dark.

### LISTEN FOR

A loud *kek-kek-kek-kek-kek*.

### COMPARE TO

American Kestrel, Peregrine Falcon, Rock Pigeon.

### NATURE NOTES

Merlins may cache excess prey in conifer branches or old crow nests and return to it later.

| RANGE | |
|---|---|
| ■ | Breeding only |
| ■ | Resident year round |
| ■ | Wintering only |

# *Falco rusticolus*

White morph                        LYNCH

Gray morph                         SMALL

THE GYRFALCON IS THE LARGEST falcon in the world and also the most northerly breeder, nesting as far as 82°N in Greenland. In winter, it may visit the Great Lakes region where it replaces its regular summer diet of ptarmigan with that of waterfowl and Rock Pigeons.

## SIZE

Length > Red-tailed Hawk
Wingspan = Red-tailed Hawk

## GRAY MORPH ADULT

Gray head with white throat • gray back and wings with faint barring • white underparts with gray barring • gray tail with narrow bands.

## WHITE MORPH ADULT

*All white head, body and tail* • dark gray spots on back and wings • may have some dark barring on belly • white tail with dark, narrow bands.

## DARK MORPH ADULT

Dark brown head with whitish throat • dark brown body and wings • dark brown underparts with whitish streaks • brown tail with dark, narrow bands.

## FLIGHT TRAITS

*Long, pointed wings,* but rounder tips than other falcons • long tail • *strong flight.*

## GRAY MORPH ADULT

White underparts and wings with gray barring • gray tail with dark, narrow bands.

White morph — SMALL

Gray morph — BECK

### WHITE MORPH ADULT

*All white underneath* • may have dark barring on belly • black wingtips • tail with narrow bands.

### DARK MORPH ADULT

Dark brown underparts and wing linings with whitish streaks • dark primaries and secondaries • dark brown tail with narrow bands.

### FIRST YEAR MORPHS

Similar to adults but more streaked underparts and darker upperparts.

Dark morph — BECK

### LISTEN FOR

Like most other falcons, a *kak-kak-kak-kak-kak*.

### COMPARE TO

Peregrine Falcon, Northern Goshawk.

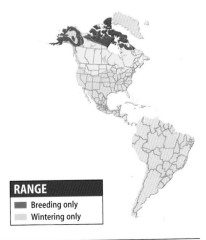

| RANGE | |
|---|---|
| ■ | Breeding only |
| ■ | Wintering only |

## *Falco peregrinus*

**Adult**

**First year**  FLYNN

IT HAS BEEN ESTIMATED THAT this falcon may reach speeds of over 200 miles per hour (320 km/h) when it is swooping or diving for prey. It also catches flying prey by level chases or by surprise attacks. The Peregrine Falcon is one of the most widely distributed birds in the world, being found across all continents except Antarctica. Because of this immense range, its prey list likely covers over 1,000 species of birds, ranging from hummingbirds and songbirds to cranes and geese. Peregrines may also take small mammals, insects and fish occasionally.

Adult WHEELER

## SIZE

Length = American Crow
Wingspan > American Crow

### ADULT

Black cap • *black mustache* • white cheek and throat • dark gray back and wings • wing tips almost reach the tip of the tail • white underparts with dark barring on belly and undertail coverts • gray tail with dark, narrow bands.

### FIRST YEAR

Buffy crown • *dark mustache* • dark patch around eye • brown back • whitish or buffy underparts with dark streaks • brown tail with dark, narrow bands.

## FLIGHT TRAITS

*Very strong, fluid flight* • when flapping, it uses a "rowing" motion • *long, very pointed wings* • long tail • soars with wings held flat.

### ADULT

Black mustache • white throat and breast • white belly, undertail coverts and wing linings with dark barring • gray tail with dark, narrow bands.

### FIRST YEAR

Dark mustache • whitish or buffy throat and breast • whitish or buffy underparts and wing linings with dark streaks on belly and wing linings • brown tail with narrow bands.

### WESTERN

First years of western Peregrines are much darker than the above description.

### LISTEN FOR

A loud *kak-kak-kak-kak-kak-kak-kak*.

### COMPARE TO

Gyrfalcon, Merlin, Northern Goshawk, Mississippi Kite, Rock Pigeon.

### NATURE NOTES

There are records of Peregrines hunting at night. Due to the efforts of many conservation groups, Peregrines are becoming more common in the Great Lakes region. Many large cities now support nesting pairs.

**RANGE**
- Breeding only
- Resident year round
- Wintering only

# Falco mexicanus

Adult                                                    LYNCH

First year                                               WHEELER

THIS WESTERN FALCON WILL hunt from perches or fly quickly close to the ground and surprise ground squirrels or small birds such as Horned Larks and Western Meadowlarks. The Prairie Falcon is rare in most of the Great Lakes region, but is considered regular in Minnesota.

### SIZE

Length = American Crow
Wingspan = American Crow

### ADULT

Thin, white eyebrow • white patch behind eye • brown head and mustache • brown back and wings • white underparts with dark speckles on breast and belly • light brown tail with faint, narrow barring.

Note the black "armpits"

WHEELER

## FLIGHT TRAITS

Wings pointed, but less so than Peregrine's • strong and swift flyer.

## ADULT

White throat, breast and belly • dark speckles on breast and belly • *light primaries, secondaries and tail feathers with faint barring* • *black "armpits" and parts of the wing linings*.

## FIRST YEAR

Similar to adult except for • dark streaks on breast and belly.

## LISTEN FOR

A shrill *kek-kek-kek-kek-kek*.

## COMPARE TO

Merlin, Peregrine Falcon, Gyrfalcon.

## RANGE

■ Breeding only
■ Resident year round
■ Wintering only

# Tyto alba

**Adult**

SMALL

THE BARN OWL IS RESPONSIBLE for many folk tales that include evil owls. Because they often nest in attics and church steeples, the human inhabitants would often hear the owls' screams and hisses late at night. It is no wonder that these frightened people thought ill of them. Yet, Barn Owls have done their share to help humans as well. It has been estimated that a 10-year-old Barn Owl would have eaten approximately 11,000 mice in its lifetime. And, calculating the amount of food these mice would have eaten if they had survived for one year, this one Barn Owl would have saved about 13,000 tons of grain or crops! No wonder they are encouraged to nest in hay lofts in many areas. Barn Owls were once much more common in the Great Lakes region, but numbers have dropped dramatically in many parts of their northern range.

### SIZE

Length = American Crow
Wingspan > American Crow

### ADULT

*White, heart-shaped face* • *dark eyes* • buffy-gold back with gray mottling and small white and black spots • *white underparts*, variably washed with buffy-gold and small black spots (females are

Adult WHEELER

Adult FLYNN

usually darker overall) • short tail • *long legs*.

## ADULT

Very pale underwings, giving the bird an overall white appearance from below.

## LISTEN FOR

Blood-curdling screams, hisses, purrs, snores and twitters.

## COMPARE TO

Snowy Owl.

## NATURE NOTES

This owl is one of the most accurate at finding prey by sound. It has been given many other names, including White Owl, Golden Owl, Church Owl, Ghost Owl, Hissing Owl, Monkey-faced Owl, Demon Owl and Phantom Owl.

### RANGE
▮ Resident year round

**Gray morph**  SMALL

**Red morph**  McCAW

"WISE MIDNIGHT HAGS! IT IS NO honest and blunt *tu-whit to-who* of the poets, but, without jesting, a most solemn graveyard ditty, the mutual consolations of suicide lovers remembering pangs and the delights of supernal love in the infernal groves. And yet I love to hear their wailing, their doleful responses, trilled along the woodside…" Thoreau (1845) certainly summed up the eerie sounds of the screech-owl, but also described them as "a loud, piercing scream, much like the whinner of a colt perchance, a rapid trill, then subdued or smothered a note or two." Eastern Screech-Owls are one of the most familiar of owls of the southern Great Lakes region and eastern North America. Check out page 111 to see how you may be able to attract one to your backyard.

### SIZE

Length < American Robin
Wingspan > Mourning Dove

### ADULT GRAY MORPH

*Ear tufts* (can be flattened and hard to see, but are usually quite prominent) • yellow eyes • thin, black border to facial disks • white eyebrows and mustache • pale yellowish green beak • *gray upperparts with dark mottling and a line of white spots on back* • some white spots on

Gray morph

SMALL

wings • white underparts with thin dark barring and streaking • short tail.

## ADULT RED MORPH

Similar to gray morph except for • gray replaced by *rich rufous*.

## ADULT BROWN MORPH

An intermediate of the first two morphs, it is similar to gray morph except for
• gray replaced by *brown*.

## ADULT

Pale underwings with a black comma at the wrist.

### LISTEN FOR

Two main calls. The tremolo is a modulating whistle that a pair uses to stay in contact with each other. The shriller, falling whinny is a territorial call.

### COMPARE TO

Long-eared Owl, Northern Saw-whet Owl.

### NATURE NOTES

For their size, Eastern Screech-Owls are fierce little predators, taking a variety of prey, including birds much larger than themselves. I watched one fly from its nesting cavity to a perch and cough up a pellet (a ball of indigestible material including bones, hair and feathers). After it left, I examined the ground below this perch and found not only more pellets, but also fish bones and crayfish claws, showing their knack for catching whatever is available.

### RANGE

Resident year round

89

## *Bubo virginianus*

**Adult with skunk**
McCAW

**Fledgling**
REAUME

THE GREAT HORNED OWL HAS AN impressive north-to-south range in the Americas. It can be found in an amazingly varied number of habitats from the sub-Arctic areas of North America all the way to southern parts of South America. Often described as the tiger of the sky, Great Horned Owls are powerful predators that take a wide variety of prey, from swans to skunks, herons to hares, Osprey to other owls and even domestic cats (yet another reason to keep your cat indoors). Major Bendire (1892, in Bent) "reports a nest that contained a mouse, a young muskrat, two eels, four bullhead catfish, a woodcock, four Ruffed Grouse, one rabbit and eleven rats. The food taken out of the nest weighed almost 18 pounds." Great Horned Owls in our area tend to focus on small rodents and Eastern Cottontails. As these prey species are often attracted to bird seed under feeders at night, many sleeping homeowners have Great Horned Owls hunting in their backyards.

### SIZE

Length > Red-tailed Hawk
Wingspan < Red-tailed Hawk

Adult

## 🦉 ADULT

*Ear tufts* (can be flattened and hard to see, but are usually quite prominent) • *orange-brown facial disks with dark border* • yellow eyes • whitish eyebrows and mustache • *white throat patch* (can be concealed) • mottled brownish gray back • buffy underparts with *thin, dark barring* • short tail.

Adult showing nictitating membrane, a protective eyelid.

## ✒ ADULT

Buffy underwings with a dark comma on wrist.

### LISTEN FOR

The common call is a deep *hooo hoo-hoo hooooooo hooooooo*.

### COMPARE TO

Long-eared Owl.

### NATURE NOTES

For such a large bird, Great Horned Owls can be incredibly silent. I did an owl prowl early one winter morning and called for a Great Horned Owl in an area where a pair usually has a territory. I never got a response, but when I turned to leave, a Great Horned Owl flew away from the bare tree I was standing under. It had come in to my calls and landed above my head without my hearing it.

### RANGE

Resident year round

## *Bubo scandiacus*

**Adult male** McCAW

**First year female** McCAW

THE SNOWY OWL IS A WELCOMED winter visitor to the Great Lakes region. A very large owl, the Snowy is a favorite bird to watch for in the open fields of agricultural areas, but may be found in cityscapes as well. Most of the "snowies" that come this far south from their high Arctic breeding areas are heavily marked first years. Sometimes, though, an almost pure white adult male Snowy Owl may be seen perched on a fence post or telephone wire. Many of these owls stay in their Arctic homes all year round, but "irruptions" may occur in the south when major northern food sources such as lemmings become scarce. Snowy Owls are true nomads; they move to where they find prey. And they can really move. One Snowy fitted with a radio transmitter moved from a point in Siberia to a point in Arctic Canada, a distance of 1,800 miles (2,900 km), in 48 days. If a high abundance of prey can't be found during the breeding season, the owls may not even attempt to nest that year.

### SIZE

Length > Red-tailed Hawk
Wingspan > Red-tailed Hawk

First year female

McCAW

### 🦉 ADULT MALE

*All white body* • most have some sparse black or dusky spots (individuals at least three to four years old may be pure white) • yellow eyes • short tail.

### 🦉 FEMALE & FIRST YEAR

Similar to adult male except for • *variable black barring on crown, back, wings, breast, belly and tail* (first year females have the most) • *facial disks still white.*

### 🦉 ADULT & FIRST YEAR

White underwings with variable barring.

### LISTEN FOR

Usually only the males hoot, a booming *hoo* or short series of hoots that has been said to be heard up to 7 miles (11 km) away. Owls on their wintering grounds may grunt or whistle.

### COMPARE TO

Barn Owl.

### NATURE NOTES

The oldest known identifiable bird species in cave art is the Snowy Owl.

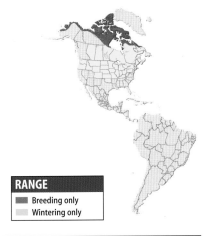

### RANGE
■ Breeding only
■ Wintering only

**Adult** McCAW

**Fledgling** McCAW

LIKE ITS NAME SUGGESTS, THIS boreal inhabitant combines owl characteristics with a hawklike body. Built for speed, the Northern Hawk Owl uses its short wings and long tail to do low, fast attacks on prey. It is also adept at listening from a perch and catching voles through a layer of snow. In winter, the Northern Hawk Owl sometimes comes south of its normal northern boreal forest home. Its mostly diurnal habits and remarkable tameness often allow birders to get very good looks.

### SIZE

Length = American Crow
Wingspan = Rock Pigeon

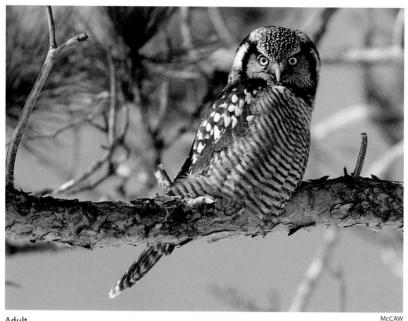

Adult                                                                McCAW

## 🦉 ADULT

Light gray or white facial disks with *thick black borders that extend to the eyes* • yellow eyes • brownish gray crown with small white spots • *white and black lines on sides of the head* • brownish back with white mottling • *white underparts with rufous or brown barring* • *long tail.*

## FLIGHT TRAITS

Fast flapping, like an accipiter, but can also hover like a kestrel.

## LISTEN FOR

A whistled trill (similar to the display "call" of a snipe).

## COMPARE TO

Cooper's Hawk, Sharp-shinned Hawk.

## NATURE NOTES

Will do a distraction "broken wing" display to lead potential predators from fledged young.

### RANGE

░ Resident year round

**Adult** SMALL

**Adult** FLYNN

THE BARRED OWL'S DARK EYES set it apart from all of the other eastern North American owls except for the Barn Owl. Their wise look prompted Thoreau (1858) to write, "Solemnity is what they express, – fit representatives of the night." An inhabitant of often densely wooded areas, the Barred Owl is equally at home in southern swampland and northern boreal forest. Its loud, distinctive hooting has enhanced many campers' evenings. These hoots can sometime evolve into a maniacal series of notes that have given rise to a variety of other names for this species, such as Crazy Owl and Laughing Owl.

Adult

## SIZE

Length > Red-tailed Hawk
Wingspan> American Crow

### 🦉 ADULT

*Dark eyes* • facial disks with brown border
• whitish or gray eyebrows and mustache
• brown upperparts with white mottling
• white or buffy underparts • *barred breast*
• *thick dark streaks on belly* • short tail.

### 🪶 ADULT

Buffy underwings with dark comma on
wrist.

### LISTEN FOR

A throaty series of deep hoots in the
pattern *Who cooks for you? Who cooks
for you-all?* Can also do a series of
laughing hoots and screams.

## COMPARE TO

Great Gray Owl.

## NATURE NOTES

This species will use specially made nest
boxes (see page 111).

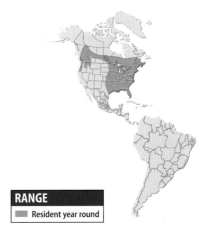

### RANGE
Resident year round

**Adult** McCAW

**Adult** McCAW

THE GREAT GRAY OWL'S LARGE size, huge facial disks and penetrating stare give it an incredible presence. They can also be quite tame, which allows observers to watch their behavior. Though birders in the northern Great Lakes area may be able to see these owls in their resident boreal forest homes, most observers must wait for the winters when some Great Gray Owls come south. These owls are the biggest looking owls in North America, but they may weigh much less than a Snowy or Great Horned Owl. Because of this difference in bulk, Great Gray Owls tend to focus more on smaller prey than these other two species. Some populations may subsist almost entirely on voles.

Adult

McCAW

## SIZE

Length < Bald Eagle
Wingspan > Red-tailed Hawk

### ADULT

*Large facial disks with dark border and thin, dark concentric circles* • *small yellow eyes* • light gray eyebrows and mustache • broken white line across throat (can be hard to see) • body gray with dusky mottling.

### ADULT

Gray underwings with no dark comma on wrist.

### LISTEN FOR

A series of evenly spaced, low, booming hoots.

### COMPARE TO

Barred Owl.

## NATURE NOTES

Great Gray Owls have been known to plunge through 1½ feet (45 cm) of snow to catch rodents that they could hear from above.

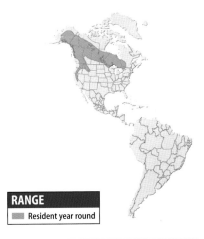

### RANGE

Resident year round

Adult      McCAW

Adult in defensive posture      FLYNN

LOOKING LIKE A MINIATURE replica of the Great Horned Owl, the Long-eared Owl can be distinguished by its smaller size, vertical black lines above and below its eyes and vertical streaks on its breast and belly. The Long-eared Owl makes quite a variety of calls. Thoreau described an encounter with a vocal owl of this species: "Just then I thought surely that I heard a puppy faintly barking at me four or five rods distant amid the bushes, having tracked me into the swamp, – what what, what what what. It was exactly such a noise as the barking of a very small dog or perhaps a fox. But it was the old owl, for I presently saw her making it."

Adult

McCAW

## SIZE

Length < American Crow
Wingspan < American Crow

### ADULT

*Long ear tufts* • yellow eyes • white
eyebrow • *orange-brown facial disks with
dark border* • *black vertical line through
eye* • mottled brownish gray back • buffy
underparts with dark barring and
*streaking* and some white mottling
(female is darker overall) • short tail.

### ADULT

Buffy underwings with a dark comma on
the wrist • similar to Short-eared Owl in
flight.

## LISTEN FOR

The male gives a series of evenly spaced,
deep hoots. This species has a wide array
of other calls that include squeals, hisses
and high-pitched barks.

## COMPARE TO

Eastern Screech-Owl, Great Horned Owl,
Short-eared Owl.

### RANGE
Resident year round

## *Asio flammeus*

**Adult** FLYNN

**Adult** FLYNN

THIS STRIKING OWL WITH THE "too much mascara" look is often out hunting at dusk or even in broad daylight. This gives us a great opportunity to watch the owl's flight pattern and its interactions with other raptors and those of its own species. Short-eared Owls often roost and hunt together in the winter months. Seeing a group of 30 to 40 owls hunting over the same fields is an incredible sight. Their mothlike flapping is interspersed with long glides as they scan and listen for small mammals. Their open field or marsh habitat is often shared with Northern Harriers and the two species may dive at one another and steal each other's prey.

Adult                                                    FAIRBAIRN

## SIZE

Length < American Crow
Wingspan = American Crow

## ADULT

Whitish or buffy facial disks • yellow eyes
• *black patch around eyes* • whitish
eyebrows • very short ear tufts that are
often hard to see • brown back and wings
with buffy or whitish mottling • *whitish or
buffy underparts with brown streaks*
(females are usually darker overall)
• short tail.

## ADULT

Whitish or buffy underwings with a dark
comma on the wrist • similar to Long-
eared Owl in flight.

## LISTEN FOR

A series of deep hoots. Also does high-
pitched barking notes and a raspy *kee-
yaaah*.

## COMPARE TO

Long-eared Owl, Northern Harrier

## NATURE NOTES

Short-eared Owls live in North America,
South America and across northern Asia
and Europe. They have also colonized
some small islands. They have been
recorded flying over the sea almost 700
miles (1,100 km) away from land.

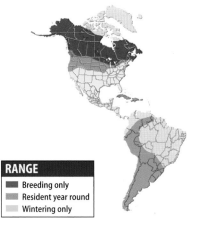

### RANGE
■ Breeding only
■ Resident year round
□ Wintering only

# *Aegolius funereus*

**Adult**  McCAW

**Fledgling**  LYNCH

LIKE THE GREAT GRAY OWL AND Northern Hawk Owl, the well-named Boreal Owl sometimes moves south of its boreal forest habitat in times of winter prey shortages. However, unlike these other two owls, the Boreal Owl usually hunts at night and hides in dense conifers during daylight hours and so it is not often seen. When this owl becomes active at night to hunt, it uses hearing to find much of its prey. The Boreal Owl has one ear opening that is higher than the other. This allows the owl to hear sounds in both a horizontal and a vertical plane, which helps it pinpoint where prey sounds are coming from. This is a great advantage when hunting in the dark or finding prey hiding under a layer of snow. In varying degrees, many other owl species have this adaptation as well, but it is most pronounced in the Boreal Owl's skull shape.

Adult

LYNCH

## SIZE

Length = American Robin
Wingspan > Mourning Dove

### 🪶 ADULT

*White or grayish facial disk with thick,
broken border that extends to the eyes on
the top and the bottom* • yellow eyes
• white eyebrows • *dark forehead with
white spots* • brown back with white spots
• white underparts with thick, mottled
streaks • short tail.

### 🪶 FLEDGLING

Dark brown head, facial disks, breast,
wings and back • *white eyebrows* • whitish
line on throat • white spots on wings
• light brown belly and undertail coverts.

### 🪶 ADULT

White wing linings.

## LISTEN FOR

A rapid series of short, hollow whistles.

## COMPARE TO

Northern Saw-whet Owl.

## NATURE NOTES

The size difference between females and
males is more pronounced in this species
than any other owl mentioned here.
Small males may weigh less than 3 ounces
(90 g) whereas large females may weigh
more than 7 ounces (200 g). Boreal Owls
often cache extra prey. In the winter,
when this cached prey freezes, the owls
must sit on the prey to thaw it out so it
can be eaten.

## RANGE

░░ Resident year round

**Adult**    McCAW

**Fledgling**    LYNCH

YOU CAN'T REALLY LOOK AT A Northern Saw-whet Owl without thinking, "Wow, is that ever cute!" These are the smallest owls in eastern North America and their tameness is astounding. I found my first one by almost hitting it with my forehead while I was ducking under a conifer branch along a hiking trail. Instead of flying away, it first stretched itself vertically, then slowly lowered its body into a ball. While I was sketching it, it turned its head in the direction of a mobbing chickadee. I slowly held up my pencil and the bird followed it back into its original position, allowing me to finish my sketch. If only more wildlife art subjects were that cooperative!

## SIZE

Length < American Robin
Wingspan = Mourning Dove

### ADULT

*Brownish streaked facial disks* • yellow
eyes • white eyebrows • *brown forehead
with short, thin white streaks* • brown back
and wings with white spots • white
underparts with thick, rufous-brown
streaks • *white undertail coverts* • short
tail.

### FLEDGLING

Dark brown head, facial disks, back, breast
and wings • *white eyebrows that join
together on forehead, forming a triangular
patch* • some white or buffy mottling on
wings • buffy-orange belly and undertail
coverts.

### ADULT

Whitish or buffy wing linings.

### LISTEN FOR

A long series of whistled toots. Also a
raspy *kreee-ah kreee-ah kreee-ah* series
that sounds similar to the sharpening of a
saw (thus, "saw-whet" owl).

### COMPARE TO

Boreal Owl, Eastern Screech-Owl.

### NATURE NOTES

Older Northern Saw-whet Owl nestlings
have been known to feed bits of food to
their younger siblings. Though tiny, these
owls can kill prey up to the size of a Rock
Pigeon.

Adult

McCAW

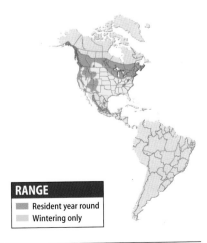

### RANGE

Resident year round
Wintering only

# Vagrants

THERE ARE OVER 40 species of birds of prey that have been recorded in the United States and Canada. The following species are rare occurrences in most of eastern North America. All of these (except Harris' Hawk) can be found in Florida.

## White-tailed Kite

*Elanus leucurus*

Adult · SMALL · Adult · WHEELER

The White-tailed Kite can be distinguished from other kites by its black shoulder patch and pure white tail. In flight, it has dark primaries and a black wrist patch. This species is usually found in the west coast states as well as southern Texas and southern Florida. In the Great Lakes region, it has been recorded in Wisconsin, Indiana and New York.

## Snail Kite

*Rostrhamus sociabilis*

Adult male · WHEELER · Adult male · WHEELER

This kite is a rare resident in parts of Florida. Its long, thin beak is used to feed on large, aquatic snails. Unlike the other kites in this book, the Snail Kite has wide, rounded wings and a black tail with a wide, white base. The adult male is shown here.

Adult                    WHEELER    Adult                    WHEELER

Harris's Hawk is a bird of the southwestern U.S., where it often teams up with others of its species to hunt cooperatively. It has bright rufous shoulders and wing linings that contrast with its dark primaries and secondaries and the black and white tail. It has been recorded in Ohio and Wisconsin.

## Short-tailed Hawk

*Buteo brachyurus*

Adult light morph        WHEELER    First year dark morph           SMALL

The Short-tailed Hawk occurs in Florida and has two morphs. Unlike other hawks in this book, the dark morph is more common than the light morph. It is a shy species that hides in forested areas and is usually only seen while it is flying.

*Caracara cheriway*

Adult WHEELER Adult SMALL

This relative of the falcons is usually found in Florida, Texas and Arizona, but has been recorded in Ontario and Minnesota. It is primarily a scavenger and can chase a single vulture off a carcass as well as steal food from buteos.

## Burrowing Owl

*Athene cunicularia*

Adult McCAW Adult SMALL

The Burrowing Owl is found over much of the western United States and southern prairie provinces, though its numbers are decreasing rapidly in some areas. It is also found in Florida. This species has been recorded in Ontario and all of the Great Lake states except Illinois and Pennsylvania.

# What can I do to help hawks & owls?

**Eastern Screech-Owl in Wood Duck box** McCAW

**Young American Kestrel in nest box** McCAW

AFTER WATCHING the aerial prowess of a flying hawk or having "talked" to a calling owl, you may be wondering what you can do to help them. Well, the fact that you use this book has already helped; your interest alone can be very beneficial to all of nature. By learning more about hawks and owls, you have become even more connected to the natural world around you. When you share your interest with others, the growing support for wildlife and their varied habitats increases.

To be more active, you could volunteer at a raptor migration site counting the spring arrivals or fall departures. Many sites, such as Hawk Mountain in Pennsylvania, Holiday Beach in Ontario or Whitefish Point in Michigan, have volunteer programs. As well, you could volunteer your time to do owl surveys for bird monitoring programs or work at a local raptor rehabilitation center.

To help with nesting sites, you could build and monitor owl or kestrel nest boxes. If you are near suitable habitat, you could build nest boxes for Barred Owls or help put up a nesting platform for Osprey. Information on how to construct and where to locate nesting boxes and platforms is available from a variety of sources including local naturalist groups, nature stores and the Wildlife Service.

# Owl prowls

Pellet of Great
Horned Owl –
shows teeth of
mouse

ONE OF MY FAVORITE birding activities is going on an owl prowl. Here are a few helpful tips on how to conduct your own.

**WHERE?**
- A wooded area bordering an old field is often a good place.
- During the day scout out good roosting areas by looking for owl pellets (regurgitated clumps of indigestible hair, bone and feathers) or white wash (owl poo on branches or tree trunks).

**WHEN?**
- It is a good idea to conduct most prowls in the winter so the owls are not disturbed during nesting.

**HOW?**
- You can use a tape recording of owl calls, but it is more fun trying to get an owl to respond from a sound that you make yourself.
- Try whistling through a bit of saliva on the back of your tongue for a really good Screech-Owl call.
- Making deep hoots in your throat will work for Great Horned and Barred Owls.
- Listen to a tape of owl calls and practice.

**ETIQUETTE**
- Once you get a good response, stop calling and listen (this makes it less stressful on the owl as it may think it has scared the "intruder" away from its territory).
- Stay still and watch for movement and silhouettes in the branches; some owls may stay silent but fly in closer to you.
- If possible, don't use a flashlight – this is a listening adventure!
- If you must use a flashlight, try to just let the edge of the beam hit the owl.

McCAW

# Author's notes

TO NATHAN, for all of our past owl prowls.

AND TO SKYE, for all our future ones.

SPECIAL THANKS to Karl Konze and Jim Coey for reviewing earlier drafts of this book. Thank you to Gareth Lind for his great design sense and to everyone at Firefly for their involvement and support. This book would not have been possible without the talent, generosity and patience of the photographers – thanks, guys!

# Credits

Photographers: Tony Beck, Scott Fairbairn, Jim Flynn, Wayne Lynch, Robert McCaw, John Reaume, Brain E. Small, Brian K. Wheeler

The range maps throughout this book were generously provided by WILDSPACE™ 2002. WILDSPACE™: digital hemispheric range maps for the breeding birds of Canada. Canadian Wildlife Service, Ontario Region, Ottawa Ontario, Canada.

# References

BECAUSE OF THE THRILL of hawk-watching and the popularity of owls, there are many great references for birders to utilize. For hawks, *A Photographic Guide to North American Raptors* by Wheeler and Clark and *Hawks in Flight* by Dunne, Sibley and Sutton are musts for the serious raptor watcher. Wheeler is also soon to come out with another guide called *Raptors of Eastern North America*, which promises to be super, too. For owls, *North American Owls: Biology and Natural History* by Johnsgard has a lot of information for those who want more detail. As well, *Owls of the World: Their Lives, Behavior and Survival* by Duncan covers many topics and is a good read. *The Birds of North America*, edited by Poole and Gill, includes heaps of information on hawks and owls that has been collected by the scientific community.

"Aging Bald Eagles," by William S. Clark, *Birding*, February 2001.

*Annotated Checklist of the Birds of Ontario, second edition* by R.D. James, 1991, Royal Ontario Museum.

*Atlas of the Breeding Birds of Ontario* by M.D. Cadman, P.F.J. Eagles and F.M. Helleiner, 1987, University of Waterloo Press.

*The Audubon Society Encyclopedia of North American Birds* by John K. Terres, 1991, Wings Books.

*The Birder's Handbook* by P.R. Ehrlich, D.S. Dobkin and D. Wheye, 1988, Fireside/Simon and Schuster Inc.

*The Birds of Canada – revised edition* by W. Earl Godfrey, 1986, National Museum of Canada.

*The Birds of North America* series published by The Academy of Natural Sciences of Philadelphia and The American Ornithologists' Union.

*Check-list of North American Birds*, 1998, by The American Ornithologists' Union.

*The Dictionary of American Bird Names*, revised edition by E.A. Choate, 1985, Harvard Common Press.

*Field Guide to the Birds of North America* by the National Geographic Society, 1987.

*Forest Raptors and their Nests in Central Ontario: A Guide to Stick Nests and their Uses*, 1998, Queen's Printer for Ontario.

*A Guide to Field Identification: Birds of North America* by C.S. Robbins, B. Bruun and H.S. Zim, 1966, Golden Books.

*Hawks in Flight* by P. Dunne, D. Sibley and C. Sutton, 1988, Houghton Mifflin Company.

*Hawks of Holiday Beach* by A. Chartier and D. Stimac, 1993, Holiday Beach Migration Conservatory.

*How to Spot Hawks and Eagles* by C. Sutton and P.T. Sutton, 1996, Houghton Mifflin Company.

*John James Audubon: Writings and Drawings*, edited by C. Irmscher, 1999, The Library of America.

*Life Histories of North American Birds of Prey*, edited by A.C. Bent, 1937 and 1938, U.S. National Museum.

"The Magic of Snowy Owls" by Lynne Warren, *National Geographic*, December 2002.

*National Audubon Society Field Guide to North American Birds – eastern region* by J. Bull and J. Farrand, Jr., 1994, Alfred A. Knopf, Inc.

*North American Owls: Biology and Natural History* by P.A. Johnsgard, 1988, Smithsonian Institute Press.

*Owls by Day and Night* by H.A. Tyler and D. Philips, 1978, Naturegraph Publishers Inc.

*Owls in Folklore and Natural History* by V. Holmgren, 1988, Capra Press.

*Owls of the World: Their Lives, Behavior and Survival* by J. R. Duncan, 2003, Firefly Books.

*Owls of the World* by R. Hume, 1991, Running Press.

*Owls: Their Natural & Unnatural History* by J. Sparks, 1970, Taplinger Publishing Company.

*Peterson Field Guides: Advanced Birding* by Kenn Kaufman, 1990, Houghton Mifflin Company.

*Peterson Field Guides: Eastern Birds* by R.T. Peterson, Houghton Mifflin.

*Peterson Field Guides: Hawks* by W.S. Clark and B.K. Wheeler, 1987, Houghton Mifflin.

*Peterson Natural History Companions: Lives of North American Birds* by Kenn Kaufman, 1996, Houghton Mifflin.

*A Photographic Guide to North American Raptors* by B.K. Wheeler and W.S. Clark, 1995, Academic Press.

*Raptors of Eastern North America* by B.K. Wheeler, 2003, Princeton University Press.

*Raptors: North American Birds of Prey* by N. and H. Snyder, 1991, Raincoast Books.

*Raptors of the World* by J. Ferguson-Lees and D.A. Christie, 2001, Houghton Mifflin Company.

*Seasonal Status of Birds: Point Pelee National Park and Vicinity* compiled by J.R. Graham, 1996.

*The Sibley Guide to Birds* by D.A. Sibley, 2000, Alfred A. Knopf.

*Stokes Behaviour Guide: Bird Behaviour Vol. 3* by Donald and Lillian Stokes, 1989, Little, Brown & Company.

*Stokes Field Guide to Birds: Eastern Region* by Donald and Lillian Stokes, 1996, Little, Brown & Company.

*Studer's Popular Ornithology: The Birds of North America* edited by J.H. Studer, 1881, Harrison House.

*Thoreau on Birds* by Henry David Thoreau, 1910, Beacon Press.

# Owl comparison chart

Great Horned Owl • page 90     McCAW

Long-eared Owl • page 100     McCAW

Eastern Screech-Owl • page 88     SMALL

Short-eared Owl • page 102     FLYNN

Northern Saw-whet Owl • page 106     McCAW

Boreal Owl • page 104     McCAW

Barred Owl • page 96

Barn Owl • page 86

Great Gray Owl • page 98

First year Snowy Owl • page 92

# Accipiter comparison chart – perched

WHEELER

**First year Sharp-shinned Hawk**

WHEELER

**First year Cooper's Hawk**

WHEELER

**First year Northern Goshawk**

WHEELER

**Adult Sharp-shinned Hawk • page 40**

FLYNN

**Adult Cooper's Hawk • page 44**

FLYNN

**Adult Northern Goshawk • page 48**

| | Head | Breast & belly | Undertail coverts | Tail shape | Tail pattern | Legs |
|---|---|---|---|---|---|---|
| **First year Sharp-shinned** | Small | White with thick brown streaks | Plain white | Long & thin with a squarish tip, outside tail feathers similar in length to the others | Thick dark bands with thin white terminal band | Long & very thin |
| **First year Cooper's** | Large | White with thin brown streaks | Plain white | Long & thin with a rounded tip, outside tail feathers shorter than the others | Thick dark bands with fairly thick white terminal band | Long & stronger looking |
| **First year Northern Goshawk** | Size in proportion to body, whitish eyebrow | Buffy or whitish with thick brown streaks | White with dark streaks | Long & broad | Thick, dark jagged bands, each with a thin white border on upper surface | Strong-looking |
| **Adult Sharp-shinned** | Small | White with thick rusty-orange barring | Plain white | Long & thin with a squarish tip, outside tail feathers similar in length to the others | Thick dark bands with thin white terminal band | Long & very thin |
| **Adult Cooper's** | Large | White with thick rusty-orange barring | Plain white | Long & thin with a rounded tip, outside tail feathers shorter than the others | Thick dark bands with fairly thick white terminal band | Long & stronger looking |
| **Adult Northern Goshawk** | Size in proportion to body, whitish eyebrow | White with very thin gray barring | Plain white | Long & broad | Thick dusky bands | Strong-looking |

Note: more than one characteristic is often needed to correctly identify accipiters.

# Accipiter comparison chart – in flight

First year Northern Goshawk

First year Cooper's Hawk

First year Sharp-shinned Hawk

| | Head | Breast & belly | Undertail coverts | Wing shape in a soar | Flapping style | Tail shape | Tail pattern |
|---|---|---|---|---|---|---|---|
| **First year Sharp-shinned** | Small | White with thick brown streaks | Plain white | Short & rounded, often pushed forward | Fast & floppy | Long & thin with a squarish tip, outside tail feathers similar in length to the others | Thick dark bands with thin white terminal band |
| **First year Cooper's** | Large, often projecting well beyond leading edge of wings | White with thin brown streaks | Plain white, often extends into lower belly | Straight, longer than others | Stiff | Long and thin with a rounded tip, outside tail feathers shorter than others | Thick dark bands with fairly thick white terminal band |
| **First year Northern Goshawk** | Size in proportion to body, whitish eyebrow | Buffy or whitish with thick brown streaks | White with dark streaks | Broad & often more pointed | Deep & buteolike | Long & broad | Thick, dark jagged bands, each with a thin white border |
| **Adult Sharp-shinned** | Small | White with thick rusty-orange barring | Plain white | Short & rounded, often pushed forward | Fast & floppy | Long & thin with a squarish tip, outside tail feathers similar in length to the others | Thick dark bands with thin white terminal band |
| **Adult Cooper's** | Large, often projecting well beyond leading edge of wings | White with thick rusty-orange barring | Plain white | Straight, longer than others | Stiff | Long and thin with a rounded tip, outside tail feathers shorter than others | Thick dark bands with fairly thick white terminal band |
| **Adult Northern Goshawk** | Size in proportion to body, white eyebrow | White with very thin gray barring | Plain white | Broad & often pointed more than others | Deep & buteolike | Long & broad | Thick dusky bands |

# Broad-winged/Red-shouldered Hawk comparison chart – in flight

First year Broad-winged

First year Red-shouldered

Adult Broad-winged • page 54

Adult Red-shouldered • page 52

| | Primary "window" | Primaries & secondaries | Wing linings | Tail shape | Tail pattern |
|---|---|---|---|---|---|
| **First year Broad-winged** | No | White with thick dusky band on trailing edge, some faint thin barring | White with some streaks | Very short | Fairly thick dark terminal band & many thin bands |
| **First year Red-shouldered** | Yes, but depends on lighting conditions | Faint black & white bars | White with some streaks | Longer | Many dark bands & thin white bands |
| **Adult Broad-winged** | No | White with thick black band on trailing edge, some faint thin barring | White with maybe some rusty barring | Very short | Two thick black bands separated by one thick white band |
| **Adult Red-shouldered** | Yes, but depends on lighting conditions | Black & white bars | White with rusty-orange barring | Longer | Black with two to three thin white bands |

# Hawk comparison chart – perched

Broad-winged Hawk • page 54 — WHEELER

Red-shouldered Hawk • page 52 — McCAW

Red-tailed Hawk • page 62 — McCAW

Rough-legged Hawk • page 68 — WHEELER

Sharp-shinned Hawk • page 40 — WHEELER

Cooper's Hawk • page 44 — FLYNN

Northern Goshawk • page 48 — FLYNN

first-year Northern Harrier • page 36 — WHEELER

SMALL

**Female American Kestrel · page 74**

SMALL

**Peregrine Falcon · page 82**

WHEELER

**First year Bald Eagle · page 32**

WHEELER

**olden Eagle · page 72**

SMALL

Light morph Swainson's Hawk • p. 58

Adult Broad-winged Hawk • p. 54

Adult Red-shouldered Hawk • p. 52

Osprey • p. 24

First year Broad-winged Hawk • p. 54

First year Red-shouldered Hawk • p. 52

Light morph Rough-legged Hawk • p. 68

First year Rough-legged Hawk • p. 68

First year Red-tailed Hawk • p. 62

Dark morph Rough-legged Hawk • p. 68

Adult Ferruginous Hawk • p. 66

Adult Red-tailed Hawk • p. 62

First year Golden Eagle • p. 72

First year Bald Eagle • p. 32

Turkey Vulture • p. 20

emale Northern Harrier • p. 36

WHEELER

First year Northern Harrier • p. 36

WHEELER

irst year Northern Goshawk • p. 48

WHEELER

First year Cooper's Hawk • p. 44

WHEELER

First year Sharp-shinned Hawk • p. 4

dult Northern Goshawk • p. 48

WHEELER

Adult Cooper's Hawk • p. 44

WHEELER

Adult Sharp-shinned Hawk • p. 40

Male Northern Harrier • p. 36

WHEELER

Adult Mississippi Kite • p. 30

WHEELER

First year Mississippi Kite • p. 30

Gyrfalcon • p. 80

BECK

Merlin • p. 78

SMALL

Female American Kestrel • p. 74

WHEELER

WHEELER

# Index